Mammalian Physiology and Behaviour

Mary Jones

Geoff Jones

Series editor: Mary Jones

CAMBRIDGE
UNIVERSITY PRESS

CAMBRIDGE UNIVERSITY PRESS

Cambridge, New York, Melbourne, Madrid, Cape Town, Singapore, São Paulo

Cambridge University Press
The Edinburgh Building, Cambridge CB2 2RU, UK

www.cambridge.org
Information on this title: www.cambridge.org/9780521797498

© Cambridge University Press 2002

First published 2002
6th printing 2005

Printed in Dubai by Oriental Press

Produced by Gecko Ltd, Bicester, Oxon

A catalogue record for this publication is available from the British Library

ISBN-13 978-0-521-79749-8 paperback
ISBN-10 0-521-79749-7 paperback

Front cover photograph: Cheetah running, South Africa; Telegraph Colour Library

NOTICE TO TEACHERS
It is illegal to reproduce any part of this work in material form
(including photocopying and electronic storage) except under the
following circumstances:

(i)   where you are abiding by a licence granted to your school or
        institution by the Copyright Licensing Agency;
(ii)   where no such licence exists, or where you wish to exceed the
        terms of a licence, and you have gained the written permission of
        Cambridge University Press;
(iii)   where you are allowed to reproduce without permission under
        the provisions of Chapter 3 of the Copyright, Designs and Patents
        Act 1988, which covers, for example, the reproduction of short
        passages within certain types of educational anthology and
        reproduction for the purposes of setting examination questions.

Contents

Introduction

Cambridge Advanced Sciences

The *Cambridge Advanced Sciences* series has been developed to meet the demands of all the new AS and A level science examinations. In particular, it has been endorsed by OCR as providing complete coverage of their specifications. The AS material is presented as a single text for each of biology, chemistry and physics. Material for the A2 year comprises six books in each subject: one of core material and one for each option. Some material has been drawn from the existing *Cambridge Modular Sciences* books; however, the majority is entirely new.

During the development of this series, the opportunity has been taken to improve the design, and a complete and thorough new writing and editing process has been applied. Much more material is now presented in colour. Although the existing *Cambridge Modular Sciences* texts do cover some of the new specifications, the *Cambridge Advanced Sciences* books cover every OCR learning objective in detail. They are the key to success in the new AS and A level examinations.

OCR is one of the three unitary awarding bodies offering the full range of academic and vocational qualifications in the UK. For full details of the new specifications, please contact OCR:

OCR, 1 Hills Road, Cambridge CB1 2EU
Tel: 01223 553311

The presentation of units

You will find that the books in this series use a bracketed convention in the presentation of units within tables and on graph axes. For example, ionisation energies of $1000\,kJ\,mol^{-1}$ and $2000\,kJ\,mol^{-1}$ will be represented in this way:

Measurement	Ionisation energy (kJ mol^{-1})
1	1000
2	2000

OCR examination papers use the solidus as a convention, thus:

Measurement	Ionisation energy / kJ mol^{-1}
1	1000
2	2000

Any numbers appearing in brackets with the units, for example $(10^{-5}\,mol\,dm^{-3}\,s^{-1})$, should be treated in exactly the same way as when preceded by the solidus, $/10^{-5}\,mol\,dm^{-3}\,s^{-1}$.

Mammalian Physiology and Behaviour – an A2 option text

Mammalian Physiology and Behaviour is all that is needed to cover the A2 biology option module of the same name. It is a brand new text which has been written specifically with the new OCR specification in mind. At the end of the book you will find a glossary of terms and answers to self-assessment questions.

This book assumes prior knowledge of the Central Concepts module, covered in *Biology 2*, and its six chapters correspond to the six module sections with the same titles.

Acknowledgements

1.5a, b, 1.11a, b, Mark Colyer; 1.7, 1.8a, b, 2.3a, 3.2a, 3.4a, 4.3, John Adds; 1.8d, © University of Zurich/ Nature & Science/Oxford Scientific Films; 1.13b, 5.2, Geoff Jones; 2.12b, Eye of Science/Science Photo Library; 2.14, Martin/Custom Medical Stock Photo/Science Photo Library; 2.16, Michael Abbey/Science Photo Library; 3.14d, Quest/Science Photo Library; 3.16, Astrid & Hanns-Frieder Michler/Science Photo Library; 4.10, Montreal Neuro. Institute/McGill University/CNRI/Science Photo Library; 4.15 © G. W. Willis/Oxford Scientific Films; 5.15, Western Ophthalmic Hospital/Science Photo Library; 6.3, J. A. L. Cooke © Oxford Scientific Films; 6.6, by permission of B. F. Skinner Foundation; 6.7, Tim Davis/Science Photo Library; 6.8, Dr. Wyne Aspey/Science Photo Library

CHAPTER 1

Mammalian nutrition

By the end of this chapter you should be able to:

1 explain what is meant by *heterotrophic nutrition*, and outline the basic principles;

2 explain what is meant by the terms *ingestion*, *digestion*, *absorption* and *egestion*;

3 distinguish between mechanical and chemical digestion;

4 state the sites of production and action, and explain the functions of: pepsin, trypsin, chymotrypsin, exopeptidases, amylases, maltase, lipase and bile salts;

5 recognise on photographs and diagrams, and by using the light microscope, the following main regions of the gut: stomach, ileum and colon;

6 describe the structure of the stomach and its functions in digestion and absorption;

7 describe the gross structure and histology of the pancreas and explain its functions as an exocrine gland;

8 describe the structure of the ileum and its functions in digestion and absorption;

9 describe the functions of the colon in absorption;

10 outline the roles of the nervous system and hormones in the control of digestion;

11 describe the specialisation of teeth and digestive systems in a cow (a ruminant) and a dog (a carnivore).

In *Biology 1*, we looked in detail at the human diet – what we need to eat and why. Humans, like all other animals (not only mammals) and all fungi, are **heterotrophs**. This means that we need to eat food containing organic molecules. These organic molecules, which include carbohydrates, fats and proteins, are our only source of energy. In contrast, **autotrophs** such as green plants do not need to take in any organic molecules at all. They obtain their energy from sunlight, and can use this energy to build organic molecules from inorganic ones. They produce carbohydrates from carbon dioxide and water, by photosynthesis (described in detail in chapter 2 in *Biology 2*) and can then use these carbohydrates, plus inorganic ions such as nitrate, phosphate and magnesium, to manufacture all the organic molecules that they require. Heterotrophs therefore depend on autotrophs for the supply of organic molecules on which they feed. Some of them feed directly on plants, while others feed further along a food chain. But eventually all of our food can be traced back to green plants, and the energy of sunlight.

In this chapter, we will consider what happens to the food we eat as it travels through the alimentary canal, and also look at the diets and digestive systems of some mammals other than humans.

An overview of digestion

In humans, as in all mammals, digestion takes place within the **alimentary canal**. This is a long tube which runs from the mouth to the anus. In an adult, it is up to 6 m long, with some parts of it coiled round and round inside the abdomen. The alimentary canal, plus other organs that secrete various substances into it – the salivary glands, liver and pancreas – make up the **digestive system** (*figure 1.1*).

The space in the middle of the alimentary canal, like the space in the middle of any tube in the body, is known as a **lumen**. The lumen of the alimentary canal runs without obstruction from one end of the body to the other. Substances can pass right through without ever entering a cell. Technically, therefore, it can be considered to be part of the outside world. In order to enter the tissues of the body, food substances must move into the cells in the wall of the canal, from where most of them pass into the blood stream. This process is called **absorption**.

In general, only small molecules and ions can be absorbed through the walls of the alimentary canal. These include water, inorganic ions such as iron and calcium, vitamins, amino acids and monosaccharides. Macromolecules such as starch and proteins cannot usually be absorbed, and they must first be broken down into small molecules – the monomers from which they are made – before absorption can take place. They are broken down by **hydrolysis** reactions, in a process called **chemical digestion**. A variety of different enzymes catalyse these reactions.

The enzymes get better access to the food materials within the alimentary canal if these materials are in small pieces, rather than large lumps. Humans – unlike some animals, such as dogs – normally chew their food before swallowing it, which helps to break up lumps of food into many smaller pieces with a larger surface area. Churning movements in the stomach also help with this. These two processes are sometimes known as **mechanical digestion**. So, mechanical digestion breaks up large pieces of food into small ones, and is followed by chemical digestion which breaks up large *molecules* of food into small ones.

The entry of food into the alimentary canal is known as **ingestion**. This is followed by digestion, and then absorption. Any food that cannot be digested, such as the cellulose in plant cell walls, cannot be absorbed either, so it passes right through the alimentary canal and out through the anus, in the form of **faeces**. The removal of faeces from the body is called **egestion**. It is important not to confuse this with *excretion*, which is the removal of waste products of metabolism (substances that are made inside cells, such as urea and carbon dioxide) from the body. The great majority of the material in faeces has never been inside a cell, so cannot ever have been part of metabolism.

Enzymes and digestion

A number of different enzymes are secreted into the alimentary canal.

epiglottis

buccal cavity
tongue
salivary gland

oesophagus

liver

gall bladder

bile duct

duodenum

small intestine { jejunum

ileum

appendix

cardiac sphincter

stomach

pyloric sphincter
pancreas
pancreatic duct

colon

large intestine

rectum

anal sphincter

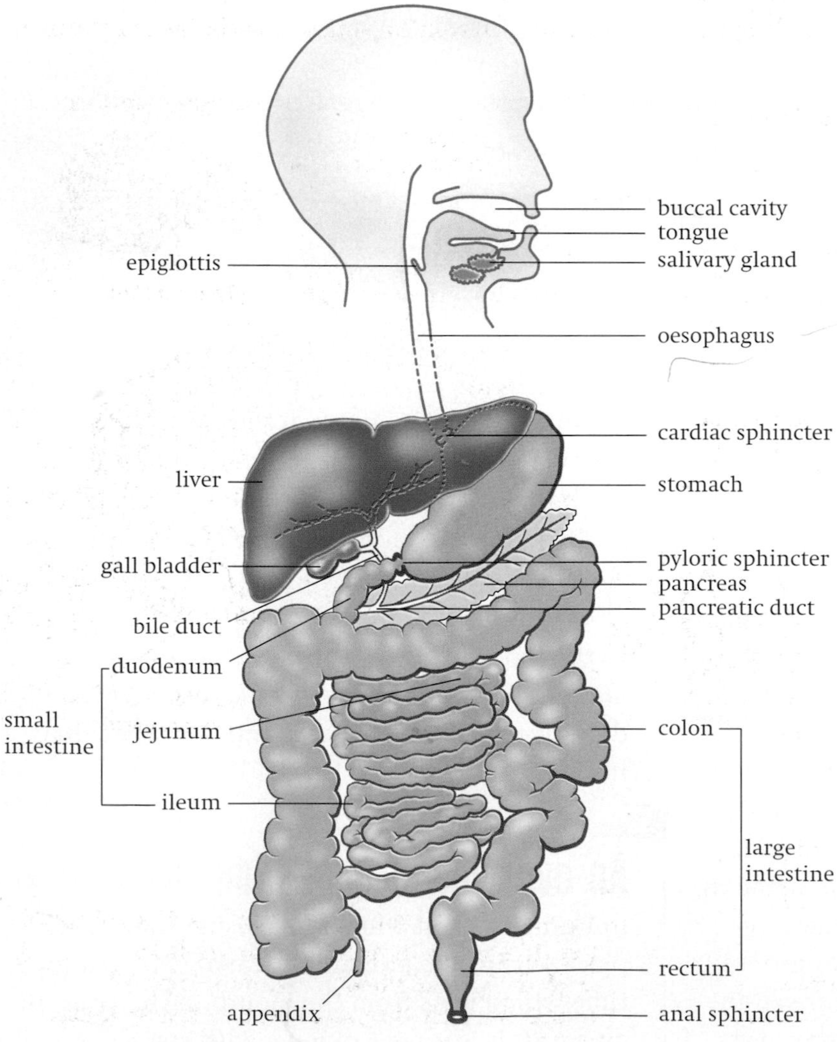

● **Figure 1.1** The human digestive system.

Before we look in detail at the events that take place within each of the sections of the alimentary canal, it may be helpful to take an overview of what these enzymes are, what they do and where they do it.

All of the reactions that take place during digestion are **hydrolysis** reactions – that is, they involve the breaking down of large molecules to small ones with the addition of water. *Figure 1.2* shows the hydrolysis reactions that occur when starch, proteins and fats are digested. All digestive enzymes are therefore **hydrolases**. They can be further classified according to the type of molecule that they break down. **Proteases** or **peptidases** catalyse the hydrolysis of proteins, **carbohydrases** the hydrolysis of carbohydrates and **lipases** the hydrolysis of lipids (*table 1.1*).

Protein digestion takes place in the stomach, duodenum and ileum. In the stomach, protein molecules are broken down into smaller lengths by the protease **pepsin**. Pepsin catalyses the hydrolysis

of some peptide bonds *within* protein molecules, so it is known as an **endopeptidase**. The result of this is therefore the breakdown of very long chains of amino acids into smaller lengths. When these arrive in the duodenum, they are acted on by two more proteases, **trypsin** and **chymotrypsin**. These two enzymes, like pepsin, are endopeptidases, breaking down the amino acid chains into even smaller lengths. These short chains are then acted on by yet another protease called **carboxypeptidase**. This behaves differently from the first three, catalysing the hydrolysis of the peptide bonds linking the end amino acids in the chain. Proteases that do this are called **exopeptidases**, and they produce single amino acids, which can then be absorbed into the blood capillaries in the walls of the small intestine.

Carbohydrate digestion begins in the mouth, where the enzyme **amylase** begins the breakdown of starch molecules into the disaccharide maltose. Nothing further happens to carbohydrates until

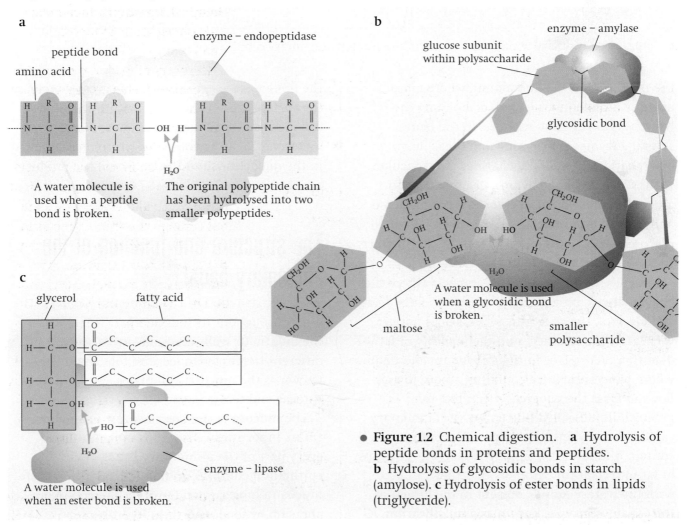

● **Figure 1.2** Chemical digestion. **a** Hydrolysis of peptide bonds in proteins and peptides. **b** Hydrolysis of glycosidic bonds in starch (amylose). **c** Hydrolysis of ester bonds in lipids (triglyceride).

Region	Secretion	Enzyme	Substrate	Product
mouth	saliva from salivary glands	amylase	starch (amylose)	maltose
oesophagus	–	–	–	–
stomach	gastric juice from gastric glands	pepsin (endopeptidase)	protein	peptides
		lipase	lipids	fatty acids and glycerol
duodenum	pancreatic juice from pancreas	amylase	starch (amylose)	maltose
		trypsin (endopeptidase)	protein	peptides
		chymotrypsin (endopeptidase)	protein	peptides
		carboxypeptidase (exopeptidase)	peptides	amino acids
		lipase	lipids	fatty acids and glycerol
	bile from liver	–	–	–
ileum	none – enzymes are produced by, and remain on the surface of, cells covering the villi	maltase	maltose	glucose
		sucrase	sucrose	glucose and fructose
		lactase	lactose	glucose and galactose
		peptidase (exopeptidase)	peptides	amino acids

Key: proteases
carbohydrases
lipases

● **Table 1.1** A summary of enzyme activity in the human alimentary canal.

the food reaches the duodenum, where more amylase is added to the food, completing the hydrolysis of starch to maltose. In the ileum, several enzymes are present that break down disaccharides to monosaccharides. In particular, **maltase** catalyses the hydrolysis of maltose to glucose; **sucrase** breaks down sucrose to glucose and fructose; and **lactase** breaks down lactose to glucose and galactose. These monosaccharides are then absorbed.

Lipid digestion begins in the stomach, where the enzyme **lipase** breaks triglycerides into fatty acids and glycerol. However, this process does not get very far in the stomach, and the majority of fat digestion takes place in the duodenum and ileum, where **pancreatic juice** containing more lipases flows in from the pancreas. Here, too, the greenish liquid called **bile** enters the alimentary canal. Bile contains no enzymes, but it does contain **bile salts** that help to disperse large drops of fat into such tiny droplets that they can mix with the watery liquids present in the lumen of the canal – a process known as **emulsification**. As

the lipases are water-soluble, this greatly increases the surface area of the lipids with which lipases can make contact. The breakdown of lipid molecules to fatty acids and glycerol is completed in the duodenum and ileum, where the products are absorbed.

The structure and function of the alimentary canal

The basic structure of the alimentary canal is the same throughout its length, apart from within the mouth. Its walls are made up of several different tissues arranged into four main layers, known as the mucosa, submucosa, muscularis externa and serosa (*figure 1.3*).

The **mucosa** is the layer nearest to the lumen. On its inner surface is a thin **epithelium**. In every part of the alimentary canal, this epithelium contains **goblet cells**, which secrete mucus to lubricate and protect the cells from abrasion by food, and from hydrolysis by

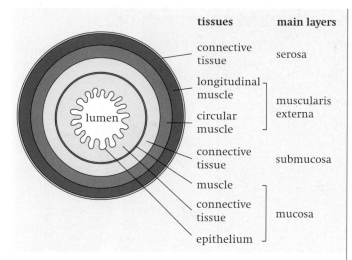

connective tissue — serosa

longitudinal muscle

circular muscle — muscularis externa

connective tissue — submucosa

muscle

connective tissue — mucosa

epithelium

lumen

● **Figure 1.3** Diagrammatic transverse section through the alimentary canal to show the tissues that make up its walls.

digestive enzymes. However, in other respects the epithelium differs considerably in different regions of the alimentary canal, as we shall see. Beneath the epithelium, still part of the mucosa, is a layer of connective tissue, and beneath that a thin layer of smooth muscle, the **muscularis mucosa**. Smooth muscle, unlike the striated or voluntary muscle that is attached to the skeleton, is not under voluntary control. It is able to contract slowly and rhythmically for long periods without tiring.

The **submucosa** is made up of connective tissue, within which lie blood vessels and nerves. The connective tissue contains a high proportion of collagen and elastin (both fibrous proteins).

The **muscularis externa**, like the muscularis mucosa, is made up of smooth muscle. Here, however, the muscle is arranged in two bands, in one of which the fibres lie lengthwise along the wall of the canal – known as **longitudinal muscle** – and in one of which they lie around the wall –

known as **circular muscle**. The contraction and relaxation of these muscles moves the food through the alimentary canal by **peristalsis** (figure 1.4) and also helps to mix the food within the canal with the various secretions, by means of churning movements.

The **serosa** is a thin layer of connective tissue that makes up the outer layer of the wall.

The mouth and oesophagus

Food is ingested into the mouth using the teeth and lips. Chewing or **mastication**, using the broad ridges and grooves on the molars and premolars, breaks solid food into smaller pieces, thus increasing its surface area.

Saliva is secreted into the mouth from three pairs of **salivary glands**. Saliva is mostly water, and this helps to dissolve any soluble components in the food, allowing them to interact with receptors in the taste buds on the tongue, so that they can be tasted. Saliva also contains mucus, which helps the tongue to form the food into a small slippery ball or bolus for swallowing, and the enzyme salivary amylase, which begins the breakdown of starch to maltose.

The action of swallowing pushes the bolus into the top of the oesophagus, and a wave of contraction and relaxation takes place along the circular and longitudinal muscles in its walls, pushing the food towards the stomach.

The stomach

The stomach is a sac with a capacity of around $5 \, dm^3$. Muscles at each end, known as **sphincters**, control the entry and exit of food to and from the stomach. When a bolus arrives at the stomach from the oesophagus, the upper, **cardiac sphincter**, relaxes to allow the food to enter. The lower, **pyloric sphincter**, remains contracted so that the food is held in the stomach for up to several hours. It then relaxes to allow the partly digested food, known as **chyme**, to pass into the duodenum.

Figures 1.5 and 1.6 (overleaf) show the structure of the stomach wall. The mucosa is very folded, forming deep pits called **gastric pits** (sometimes called **gastric glands**) which secrete a liquid

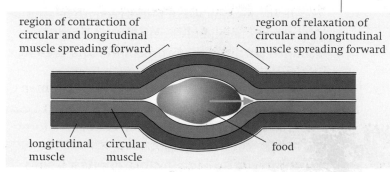

region of contraction of circular and longitudinal muscle spreading forward

region of relaxation of circular and longitudinal muscle spreading forward

longitudinal muscle   circular muscle   food

● **Figure 1.4** Peristalsis.

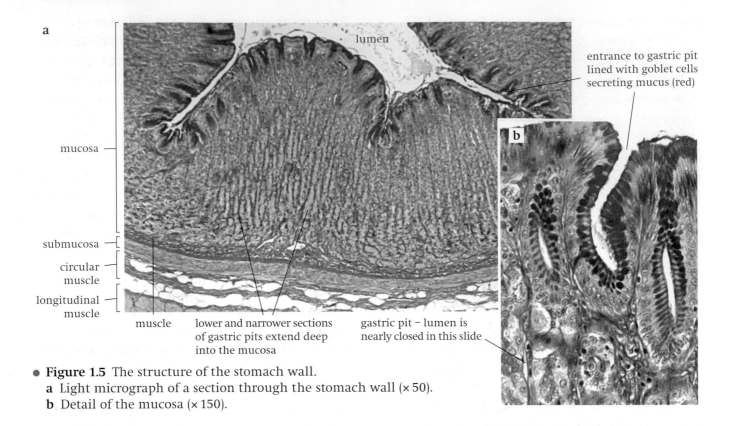

a

lumen

mucosa

submucosa

circular muscle

longitudinal muscle

muscle

lower and narrower sections of gastric pits extend deep into the mucosa

gastric pit – lumen is nearly closed in this slide

entrance to gastric pit lined with goblet cells secreting mucus (red)

b

● **Figure 1.5** The structure of the stomach wall.
  a Light micrograph of a section through the stomach wall (× 50).
  b Detail of the mucosa (× 150).

known as **gastric juice**. The epithelium of the mucosa (that is the surface layer of cells that make up the stomach wall including the gastric glands) is made up of columnar cells.

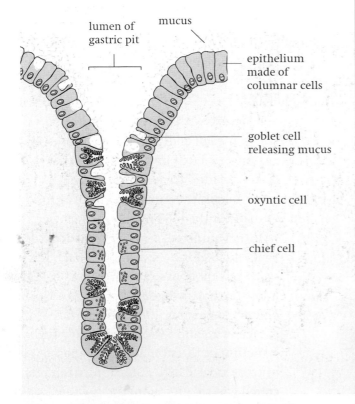

lumen of gastric pit

mucus

epithelium made of columnar cells

goblet cell releasing mucus

oxyntic cell

chief cell

● **Figure 1.6** A gastric pit in the stomach wall.

Digestion in the stomach

Gastric juice, like all the fluids secreted into the alimentary canal, is mostly water. It contains **hydrochloric acid**, which is secreted by cells in the epithelium known as **oxyntic** (sometimes called **parietal**) **cells**. These are recognisable by their numerous mitochondria, and the deep invaginations on their surface. This acid gives gastric juice a pH of 1.0 or even less, which is extremely acidic. The acidic environment of the stomach kills a high proportion of the bacteria that may be present in food.

Other cells in the epithelium, known as **chief cells**, secrete a precursor of the protease **pepsin**, known as **pepsinogen**. Pepsinogen does not function as an enzyme, and is converted to active pepsin by the removal of a short length of amino acids from one end of the molecule. This is achieved partly by the hydrochloric acid present in the stomach, and also by pepsin itself.

SAQ 1.1
Suggest why pepsin is secreted in an inactive form.

Gastric juice also contains **lipase**, which begins the breakdown of triglycerides. Both pepsin and gastric lipase have an optimum pH of well below 7, as they are adapted to function in the acidic conditions of the stomach contents.

The very acidic environment, and the presence of proteases and lipases, present a considerable hazard for the cells of the epithelium of the stomach wall. Protection is provided by the secretion of **alkaline mucus** by goblet cells within the columnar epithelium – so much of it that the whole stomach wall is coated with it. The alkalinity is produced by hydrogencarbonate ions that are secreted along with the mucus.

Absorption in the stomach

The stomach is not adapted for absorption, and none of the major nutrients – carbohydrates, fats or proteins – are absorbed through its walls.

However, there are a few substances that can be absorbed here. They tend to be substances with small, lipid-soluble molecules. One of these is **alcohol**. It can pass through plasma membranes very easily, and some can even be absorbed in the mouth if it is held there long enough. Some medicinal drugs, too, can be absorbed through the stomach wall, including **aspirin**. Unfortunately, taking high doses of aspirin regularly can damage the stomach walls, leading to the development of raw, painful and potentially dangerous ulcers in some people.

The liver and pancreas

The mix of partly-digested food, enzymes and hydrochloric acid passes into the **small intestine** when the pyloric sphincter muscle relaxes. As this happens, juices from two glands – the liver and the pancreas – also flow into the small intestine.

The **liver** is the largest gland in the body. It has many functions, which are described in Chapter 2. One of these functions is the production of **bile**, which is directly concerned with digestion. Bile secreted by the liver is stored in the **gall bladder**, and then carried along the **bile duct** into the duodenum.

Bile contains several salts derived from cholesterol, including **sodium glycocholate** and **sodium taurocholate**. These salts help to emulsify fats, breaking fat droplets in the lumen of the small intestine into tiny globules only 0.5 μm to 1.0 μm in diameter. These tiny fat particles disperse into the watery fluids in the intestine. As the food continues on its way along the intestine, a high proportion of the bile salts are absorbed into the blood, eventually finding their way back to the liver. The liver re-secretes them into the bile, and so the cycle continues. One molecule of glycocholate or taurocholate may go round and round like this many times a day.

Bile also contains **hydrogencarbonate ions**, which help to neutralise the acidic mixture of enzymes and partly-digested food entering the duodenum from the stomach.

The **pancreas** is very different in both appearance and function from the liver. Its histology (the structure and arrangement of the tissues within it) is shown in *figure 1.7*.

The pancreas is both an endocrine and exocrine gland. Endocrine glands secrete hormones directly into the blood, while exocrine glands secrete other substances into a duct. The endocrine function of the pancreas is the secretion of the hormones insulin and glucagon (*Biology 2*, page

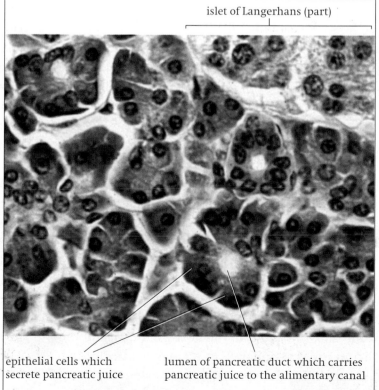

islet of Langerhans (part)

epithelial cells which secrete pancreatic juice

lumen of pancreatic duct which carries pancreatic juice to the alimentary canal

● **Figure 1.7** Light micrograph of pancreatic tissue (× 580).

101) which control blood glucose levels. This is done by cells in the islets of Langerhans. Its exocrine function is the secretion of **pancreatic juice** into the **pancreatic duct**, which empties into the duodenum.

Pancreatic juice contains a number of enzymes and enzyme precursors. Two proteases, trypsin and chymotrypsin, are secreted in an inactive form, as **trypsinogen** and **chymotrypsinogen**. Trypsinogen will gradually change into trypsin in solution, but this process of activation is speeded up when it comes into contact with another enzyme called **enterokinase**, which is secreted by cells in the wall of the duodenum. Enterokinase removes a short chain of amino acids from the two enzyme precursors, converting them to their active forms. Trypsin can also do this itself, acting on its own precursor, and also the precursor of chymotrypsin, to activate them.

Other enzymes in pancreatic juice include **carboxypeptidase**, **lipase** and **amylase**. Carboxypeptidase is yet another enzyme that is secreted in an inactive form, and is activated when trypsin removes part of its molecule. We will look at the functions of these enzymes in the next section.

Pancreatic juice also contains **hydrogencarbonate ions**. Their function is to neutralise the very acidic mixture of food and gastric juice that flows into the duodenum. All of the enzymes that act in the duodenum and ileum have optimal pHs of neutral or just above.

The small intestine

The small intestine, despite its name, is the longest part of the human alimentary canal, and can be as much as 5 m long. Its name derives from its relatively small diameter compared with other parts of the canal.

The small intestine can be considered to be made up of three different regions – the **duodenum**, **jejunum** and **ileum**. The duodenum makes up the first 25 cm or so of the small intestine, the jejunum the next 2 m or so, and the ileum the remainder. Both the pancreatic duct and the bile duct open into the duodenum.

Figure 1.8 shows the structure of the ileum wall. The most striking feature is the numerous tiny folds, known as **villi**. These are made up of the mucosa layer – that is the epithelium, connective tissue and muscularis mucosa. Each villus is about 1 mm tall, visible with the naked eye, so that if you looked at the inside of the ileum wall it would look rather like velvet. The villi provide an enormous surface area through which, as we shall see, absorption can take place. Each individual epithelium cell on a villus has its own **microvilli**, tiny folds in its surface that increase the surface area even more and that are known as a **brush border**. Each microvillus is about 1 μm long and 0.1 μm wide. The smooth muscle in the muscularis mucosa inside each villus can contract and relax to make the villi sway around, bringing them into good contact with the food in the lumen of the small intestine. Each villus contains a network of blood capillaries, and also a lymphatic capillary, important for the absorption and transport of digested food.

Between the villi are glands known as **crypts of Lieberkühn**. The crypts contain goblet cells that secrete mucus, **Paneth cells** whose function is not known for certain but which may destroy pathogens in the intestine by phagocytosis, and also many undifferentiated cells. These undifferentiated cells divide rapidly, producing new cells to replace old and damaged ones on the surfaces of the villi. In humans, the whole population of cells in the epithelium of the villi is replaced every six days. The newly-produced cells gradually work their way up to the tip of a villus, from where they are shed into the lumen. Presumably their contents can be digested and absorbed into the blood.

Digestion in the small intestine

The various enzymes in the pancreatic juice that flows into the duodenum continue to act on their substrates as the food passes from the duodenum and into the ileum. Protein molecules are hydrolysed first to peptides and then amino acids by trypsin, chymotrypsin and carboxypeptidase, lipids are hydrolysed to fatty acids and glycerol by lipases, and starch is broken down to maltose by amylase.

However, the lumen of the small intestine is by no means the only place where digestion is taking place. Many of the enzymes that act in the ileum do so while actually attached to the surface of the

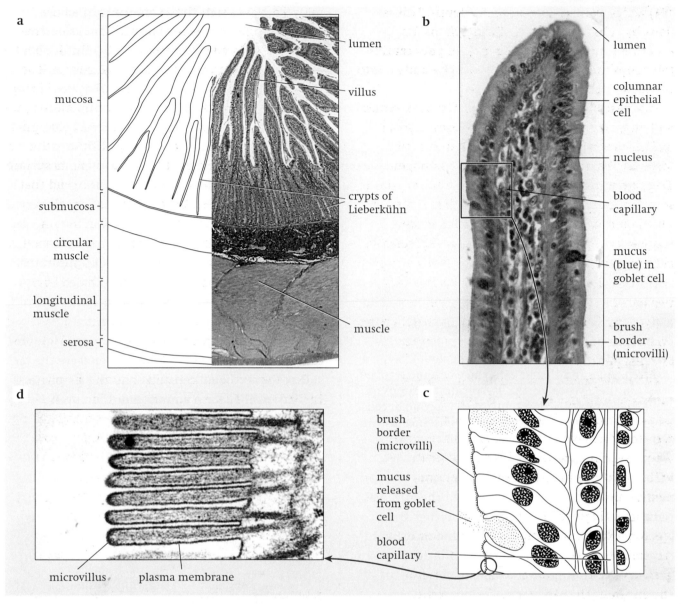

a mucosa
submucosa
circular muscle
longitudinal muscle
serosa

lumen
villus
crypts of Lieberkühn
muscle

b lumen
columnar epithelial cell
nucleus
blood capillary
mucus (blue) in goblet cell
brush border (microvilli)

d microvillus plasma membrane

c brush border (microvilli)
mucus released from goblet cell
blood capillary

● **Figure 1.8** The structure of the wall of the ileum. **a** Light micrograph of a transverse section of part of the ileum (× 35). **b** Light micrograph of a longitudinal section through a villus (× 520). **c** Diagram of part of the villus surface. **d** Electron micrograph of the surface of an epithelial cell of a villus, showing microvilli (× 70 000).

epithelial cells of the villi. Some of the enzymes from pancreatic juice, for example amylase, become adsorbed onto (that is, attached to the surface of) these cells, where they become en-tangled within the carbohydrate chains of glycoproteins in their plasma membranes (*figure 1.9, overleaf*). This is an efficient way of ensuring that the products of digestion are concentrated right next to the cells that will absorb them.

Another source of enzymes in the ileum is the epithelial cells of the villi themselves. Their plasma membranes contain several different enzymes, held in the membrane with their active sites exposed to the outside of the cell. These enzymes include exopeptidases that produce amino acids from peptides, and carbohydrases such as maltase, that produce monosaccharides from disaccharides. Overall, it appears that only a very small proportion of digestion in the ileum takes place in the lumen – the great majority of it happens right next to the plasma membranes of the epithelial cells.

Absorption in the small intestine

The final products of digestion – amino acids, fatty acids and glycerol, and monosaccharides

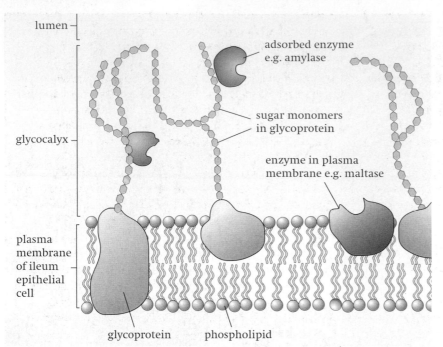

- **Figure 1.9** Digestive enzymes in the ileum. Some of the enzymes from pancreatic juice become trapped within the glycocalyx (the carbohydrate groups of the membrane glycoproteins) of the epithelial cells of the villi. There are also digestive enzymes within the plasma membranes of these cells.

such as glucose – can all cross the plasma membranes of the epithelial cells on the villi, pass right through these cells and enter either the blood capillaries (in the case of amino acids and monosaccharides) or lymphatic capillaries (products of fat digestion). Some of this absorption takes place by diffusion, some by facilitated diffusion, and some by active transport.

Glucose is mostly absorbed by a type of active transport. Sodium ions are continually pumped out of the base of the epithelial cells into the surrounding tissue fluid, using energy from the breakdown of ATP, against their concentration gradient. As a result, the concentration of sodium ions outside the cells is much greater than inside. Sodium ions from the lumen of the ileum are then allowed to diffuse across the membrane into the cell down their concentration gradient, carrying glucose molecules with them (*figure 1.10*). This is known as **cotransport**, because the movement of sodium and glucose takes place together.

Amino acids are also absorbed by active transport, mostly by cotransport with sodium ions. In young ruminants (page 14) and rodents,

significant amounts of whole protein molecules can also be absorbed, especially immunoglobulins (*Biology 1*, page 224) present in colostrum – the rich first milk produced by a lactating mother.

Fatty acids and *glycerol*, being lipid-soluble, are able to diffuse easily through the phospholipid bilayer of the plasma membranes. Once inside an epithelial cell, they are converted back to triglycerides on the smooth endoplasmic reticulum, and then transferred to the Golgi apparatus, where they are surrounded by a protein coat to form a little ball called a **chylomicron**. (Chylomicrons are a type of lipoprotein, described on page 21.) These then leave the far side of the epithelial cell and enter the lymphatic capillaries. They form a milky emulsion in the

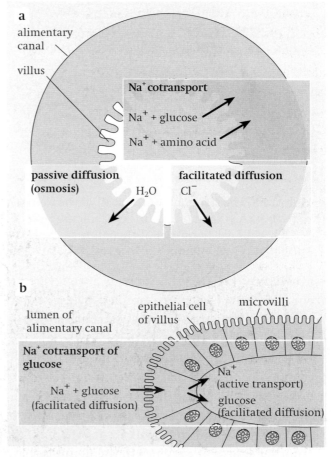

- **Figure 1.10** Absorption in the ileum.
  a Summary of the absorption mechanisms for glucose, amino acids, chloride ions and water.
  b How sodium–glucose cotransport takes place.

Box 1A Vitamins and absorption

The mechanisms of absorption of the water-soluble vitamins (that is the B vitamins, vitamin C, folic acid and nicotinic acid) and the fat-soluble vitamins (that is vitamin A and vitamin D) are rather different from one another.

Water-soluble vitamins pass through the plasma membranes of the epithelial cells of the villi by means of transport proteins. Their transport may be passive, by facilitated diffusion, or by active transport.

The uptake of vitamin B_{12} has a special mechanism. Before it can be absorbed, it must combine with a protein called **intrinsic factor**. Intrinsic factor is normally secreted in gastric juice, and the vitamin B_{12}–intrinsic factor complex forms in the stomach. It travels on until it reaches the ileum, where the plasma membranes of the epithelial cells contain a receptor that this complex can bind with. The vitamin B_{12} is then moved by active transport into the cell.

In some people, intrinsic factor is not secreted. This happens when the mucosa lining the stomach stops functioning, so that no pepsin, hydrochloric acid or intrinsic factor is secreted. This is probably an autoimmune illness, where the person's own immune system attacks the epithelial cells in the stomach. The lack of pepsin is not a problem, because proteins are still efficiently digested in the duodenum and ileum, but the lack of intrinsic factor means that vitamin B_{12} cannot be absorbed, and the person develops a disease called **pernicious anaemia**. Vitamin B_{12} is required for the normal development of red blood cells, and without it the person suffers a lack of these cells, and therefore an insufficient supply of oxygen to the tissues.

While the water-soluble vitamins must enter the epithelial cells through transporter proteins, this is not so for the fat-soluble vitamins, which can easily pass through the phospholipid bilayer by diffusion. Vitamin D also helps calcium ions to be absorbed. It seems that it acts by activating a gene in the nucleus of each epithelial cell that codes for the transporter protein that allows calcium ions to pass through the plasma membrane. If a person lacks vitamin D, they cannot absorb calcium ions, and suffer from the disease rickets (*Biology 1*, page 169).

lymph inside these capillaries, from which these lymph vessels have acquired their name **lacteals** ('lact' means 'to do with milk').

Water, *inorganic ions* and *vitamins* are also absorbed in the ileum. Fat-soluble vitamins, that is vitamins A, D and E, cross the plasma membranes easily, by diffusion. Others, and all inorganic ions, pass through transport proteins, either by facilitated diffusion or active transport. Water moves passively down its water potential gradient, by osmosis.

The colon

The colon, the caecum and appendix, and the rectum together make up the **large intestine**. The colon is around 150 cm long, and the rectum about 12 cm.

The structure of the wall of the colon is shown in *figure 1.11*. Unlike the small intestine, there are no villi. However, the inner surface is folded, and this provides a relatively large surface area for absorption. The epithelium contains columnar cells with microvilli (a brush border) which are involved in absorption, and large numbers of goblet cells that secrete copious amounts of alkaline mucus.

The function of the colon is to absorb inorganic ions and water. The ions are mostly absorbed by active transport, while water diffuses down a water potential gradient. A high proportion of water will already have been absorbed in the small intestine, but much of what remains is absorbed here.

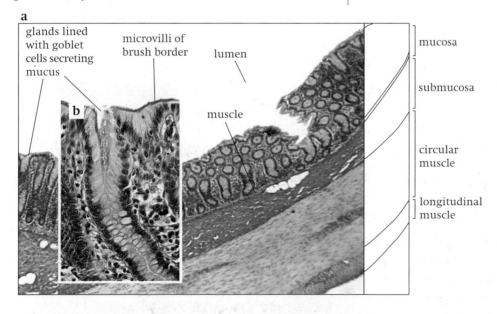

a

glands lined with goblet cells secreting mucus

microvilli of brush border

lumen

b

muscle

mucosa

submucosa

circular muscle

longitudinal muscle

- **Figure 1.11** The structure of the wall of the colon.
  a Light micrograph of a transverse section through part of the colon (× 50).
  b Detail of the mucosa (× 250).

In humans, the caecum and appendix have no function. They are said to be **vestigial** organs – that is organs that had a function in a distant ancestor of our species but now are useless. In some other mammals, such as rabbits, the caecum contains dense populations of bacteria that are able to digest cellulose.

The material that still remains inside the alimentary canal after passing through the colon is made up of indigestible material – mostly cellulose and lignin from plant cell walls – plus mucus and cells that have been shed from the surface of the canal. This material is passed periodically into the rectum and out through the anus, as **faeces**.

The control of digestion

It would clearly be very wasteful if organs such as the stomach secreted digestive fluids all the time. The timing of the release of secretions from the various regions of the alimentary canal and its associated glands is controlled by the nervous system, and also by hormones.

Control by the nervous system

The sight, smell and chewing of food can trigger the secretion of saliva from the salivary glands. This is a reflex action (*Biology 2*, page 107), in which action potentials travel from sense organs such as the eyes and nose, to the central nervous system, and then along motor neurones to the salivary glands. Pavlov's experiments with dogs (page 86) showed that they could be conditioned to associate hearing a bell ringing with food, so that the sound of the bell would trigger this same reflex action.

The part of the brain involved in the salivation reflex is the medulla oblongata (page 61). The nerves that carry impulses from here, via the spinal cord, to the salivary glands are part of the autonomic nervous system (page 51), and both parasympathetic and sympathetic nerves help to stimulate salivary secretion.

The secretion of gastric juice into the stomach is also partly controlled by the nervous system. Once again, the sight and smell of food can be stimuli for this reflex action. Nerve impulses are carried to the stomach from the brain along the **vagus nerve**, which is part of the parasympathetic nervous system (page 53). The arrival of these impulses directly stimulates the secretion of gastric juice, and also initiates the release of the hormone gastrin, as described below.

Control by the endocrine system

The secretion of digestive juices by the stomach and pancreas, and the release of bile from the gall bladder, are controlled by hormones.

The arrival of action potentials at the stomach wall, along the vagus nerve, causes the secretion of a hormone called **gastrin** by some of the cells in the mucosa. This hormone is released into the blood, and it affects the behaviour of the gastric glands, causing them to release large quantities of gastric juice. The presence of food in the stomach has a similar effect. This control mechanism therefore ensures that the stomach already contains some digestive juices when food is first swallowed, and that the quantity of these juices increases when the food actually arrives.

The secretion of pancreatic juice is largely controlled by the arrival of food in the duodenum. Contact with acidic substances stimulates cells in the wall of the duodenum to secrete a hormone called **secretin**. This, like all hormones, is released into the blood, which distributes it to its target cells in the pancreas. Secretin stimulates the exocrine cells in the pancreas to release a juice rich in hydrogen-carbonate ions, into the pancreatic duct.

The cells lining the duodenum also respond to the arrival of food containing the products of fat and protein digestion. In these circumstances they secrete a different hormone, **cholecystokinin** or **CCK** for short. CCK, like secretin, acts on the exocrine cells of the pancreas, except that this time it stimulates the secretion of a juice rich in enzymes. CCK also affects the gall bladder, causing smooth muscles in its walls to contract and force bile along the bile duct into the duodenum.

SAQ 1.2
Explain how the secretion of secretin and CCK in response to different stimuli helps to make digestion in the duodenum more efficient.

Digestion in herbivores and carnivores

Humans have evolved as **omnivores**, and our digestive system is adapted to deal with a mix of animal-derived and plant-derived material in our diet. Other mammals eat less varied diets, and have evolved digestive systems with structures and functions that are better able to deal efficiently with a purely carnivorous or herbivorous diet. We will look at one example of a carnivore, and one example of a herbivore, to see how their digestive systems differ from ours.

The dog – a carnivore

Dogs are meat-eating animals. Wild members of the dog family, such as wolves, are predators. They hunt and kill other animals which they then eat.

Figure 1.12 shows the structure of a dog's skull. The long, pointed teeth near the front of the mouth, the **canines**, are particularly noticeable. The top and bottom canines thrust past each other as the jaw is closed, allowing the dog to pierce the body of its prey with considerable force, and kill it. Behind the canines, you can see that the **premolars** and **molars** have sharp edges, and are sometimes known as **carnassial teeth**. They slice past each other as the jaw is closed. This scissor-like action can crack and crush bones, and cut meat into pieces which can then be swallowed. The small **incisors** at the front of the dog's mouth are little used in feeding, perhaps helping sometimes with scraping meat from the surface of bones. They are, however, useful in grooming fur.

Dogs scarcely chew their food at all, keeping it in the mouth only long enough to chop it into pieces small enough to be swallowed. As meat contains no starch, there is no need for amylase to be secreted, and no chemical digestion takes place in the mouth. However, the stomach contains even more concentrated acid than in humans, allowing dogs to eat what we would consider very rotten and dangerous food without harm. As in humans, pepsin in the stomach breaks down proteins. Secretions from the gall bladder and pancreas are also similar to those in the human gut.

The meat in a dog's diet is, of course, made up of animal cells. They have no cell walls, and it is therefore easy for proteases and lipases to digest their plasma membranes and then the contents of the cytoplasm. Hence there is little need to chew food – the strong acid in the stomach plus the enzymes there quickly break down the cells in the swallowed food.

SAQ 1.3
Look at your own teeth in a mirror, and draw up a table to compare the number, shape and function of each type of tooth in yourself and a dog.

SAQ 1.4
Suggest why it is a positive advantage to predators such as dogs not to chew their food before swallowing it.

The cow – a herbivore

Cows are adapted to feed on a diet of green plants, such as grass. *Figure 1.13* overleaf shows the skull of a cow, and you should immediately see many differences between that and the skull in *figure 1.12*.

In contrast to the diet of a carnivore, the food that a cow eats is made up of cells surrounded by cellulose cell walls. No mammal is able to make an enzyme that digests cellulose. The nutrients inside the cells are almost unavailable to humans, as we have no

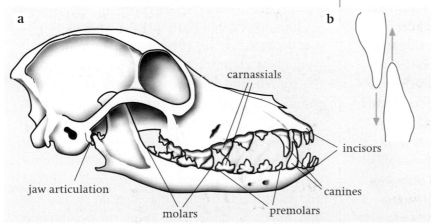

● **Figure 1.12** Dentition of a dog. **a** Side view of skull. **b** Detail to show action of carnassial teeth.

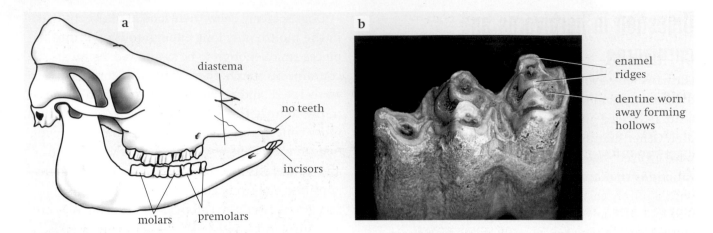

● **Figure 1.13** Dentition of a cow.   **a** Side view of skull.   **b** Surface of a premolar.

enzyme that can break down the cell walls. Moreover, much of the energy value in plant food is in the cellulose molecules themselves.

SAQ 1.5

From your knowledge of the structure of carbohydrates, and the properties of enzymes, suggest why the enzyme amylase is able to break down starch but not cellulose.

The cow has no long, pointed canines. Indeed, it has no canines at all, just a gap where you would expect them to be, known as a **diastema**. This gap enables the long, flexible tongue to move grass around in the mouth, bringing it into different positions on the teeth so that it can be thoroughly chewed from all angles. The chewing is done by premolars and molars. Instead of the sharp edges of a dog's molars, those of a cow have broad surfaces with ridges and cusps. The ridges of the teeth on the upper jaw fit into the cusps of those on the lower jaw, and *vice versa*. Grass lying between these teeth is ground thoroughly, as the cow's jaw moves from side to side while it chews. The bone structure and musculature of the cow's lower jaw allows this side to side movement, whereas that of a dog results in a crisp up and down chopping movement.

The cow does have incisors on its lower jaw; they are shaped like chisels and point forward. There are no incisors on the upper jaw, only a horny pad. If you have a chance to watch a cow feeding, notice how it tears off mouthfuls of grass using its tongue, its incisors and the horny pad above that they can bite against.

One further difference between the teeth of a cow and of a dog is that, while a cow's teeth continue to grow throughout life, a dog's teeth do not. The roots of a cow's teeth remain open, allowing blood to continue to enter the teeth and supply the living cells within with oxygen and nutrients, allowing growth. In contrast, the roots of a dog's teeth become closed, preventing further growth once the teeth are fully formed. The need for continual growth of teeth in a herbivore arises because the teeth surfaces are continually ground down by chewing, whereas those of a carnivore tend to remain relatively undamaged.

While the differences between the teeth of a cow and those of a human and dog are considerable, there are even greater differences in the structure of their stomachs. *Figure 1.14* shows the stomach of a cow. Only the **abomasum** is the equivalent of the stomach of a human or dog. The other three chambers have no counterpart in the human or canine digestive system.

This complicated structure has evolved in this way because it helps the cow to obtain nutrients from plant material. Inside the largest chamber, the **rumen**, and also the **reticulum**, there is a community of anaerobic microorganisms. They are able to produce enzymes which break down cellulose to the disaccharide cellobiose and the monosaccharide glucose. Other enzymes then convert these sugars to fatty acids, releasing carbon dioxide and methane as they do so. The carbon dioxide and methane go up the oesophagus and into the air around the cow, while the fatty acids are absorbed through the walls of the rumen. Many of the tissues in a cow's body are adapted to use fatty acids rather than glucose as their main respiratory substrate.

This system only works well if the plant material arriving in the rumen is well-chewed, with a large surface area and some of its cell walls broken down by mechanical digestion in the mouth. Periodically, some of the contents of the rumen and reticulum pass back up the oesophagus into the mouth, where they are chewed again before being re-swallowed. Cows spend many hours chewing the cud in this way.

Material from the rumen and reticulum eventually passes on to the omasum and abomasum. With the food go millions of the microorganisms from the rumen and reticulum. The abomasum, like a human's or dog's stomach, secretes hydrochloric acid and proteases, which digest the proteins in the microorganisms. The microorganisms will have made these proteins using the carbohydrates in the cow's food, plus some kind of nitrogen source, of which the main one is **urea**. Copious quantities of saliva are secreted from the cow's salivary glands – up to 100 dm^3 per day – and this saliva contains considerable amounts of urea, which has been formed in the liver by the deamination of amino acids. Much of this urea is reconverted to amino acids and then proteins by the bacteria in the rumen. The bacterial proteins

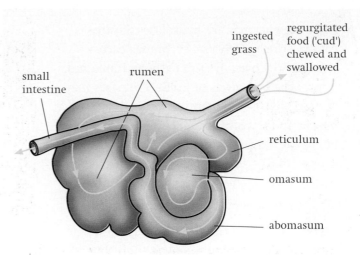

● **Figure 1.14** The structure of the rumen and associated organs in a cow.

are digested to amino acids in the abomasum, and absorbed by the cow; some of these amino acids will be used to form more urea in the liver, so that a kind of 'internal nitrogen cycle' takes place via the cow's salivary glands, saliva, stomach, blood, liver and salivary glands again. Many cattle feeds also contain urea, to maximise the production of proteins in the rumen, and hence increase the protein available to the cow. Thus the microorganisms in the rumen are the main source of protein in the natural diet of a cow, although industrially-produced cattle feed may contain other protein sources such as fish meal.

SUMMARY

◆ Heterotrophs are organisms that require organic molecules in their diet, in contrast to autotrophs such as green plants, that synthesise organic molecules from inorganic ones. All animals and fungi are heterotrophs.

◆ In mammals, the digestive system is made up of the alimentary canal and associated organs, namely the salivary glands, liver and pancreas.

◆ Food has to be broken down into small molecules before it can be absorbed. This is digestion. Mechanical digestion is the use of mechanical processes, such as chewing in

the mouth and churning in the stomach, to break large pieces of food into small ones. Chemical digestion is the breakdown of large molecules to small ones, by hydrolysis reactions that are catalysed by enzymes.

◆ The taking of food into the alimentary canal is known as ingestion. It is followed by digestion and then absorption, which is the transfer of digested food from the lumen of the alimentary canal into the blood stream. Undigested food passes out of the alimentary canal through the anus, a process known as egestion.

◆ Digestive enzymes are hydrolases. Proteases catalyse the hydrolysis of proteins, carbohydrases the hydrolysis of carbohydrates and lipases the hydrolysis of lipids. Proteases may be classified as endopeptidases (such as pepsin and trypsin) which break peptide bonds within a protein molecule, and exopeptidases (such as carboxypeptidase) which break the terminal peptide bonds.

◆ The wall of the alimentary canal is made up of four layers; the inner one is the mucosa, then the submucosa, then the muscularis externa and finally the serosa on the outer surface. Throughout the alimentary canal, the mucosa contains goblet cells that secrete mucus. The muscularis externa contains smooth muscle, which is reponsible for moving food through the alimentary canal by peristalsis, and also churning movements which mix food with enzymes.

◆ The stomach wall contains deep gastric glands, which secrete gastric juice. This contains hydrochloric acid, lipase and a precursor of pepsin, pepsinogen. Pepsin is an endopeptidase. Absorption in the stomach is confined to small, lipid-soluble molecules such as alcohol, plus a few other substances such as aspirin.

◆ The small intestine is made up of the duodenum, jejunum and ileum. Pancreatic juice, containing endopeptidases, exopeptidases, lipase, amylase and hydrogencarbonate ions, flows into the duodenum. Bile, containing bile salts that emulsify fats, is secreted by the liver and stored in the gall bladder before flowing into the duodenum. The wall of the small intestine is made up of many villi, whose epithelial cells have microvilli on their surfaces. Most digestion in the ileum takes place at the surface of these cells. The products of digestion are then absorbed through these cells, by diffusion, facilitated diffusion and active transport, into the capillaries and lymphatic capillaries inside the villi.

◆ The colon has folded walls, but no villi. Absorption of most of the water remaining in the food, and also of inorganic ions, takes place here.

◆ The secretion of digestive juices is controlled by reflex actions, and also the secretion of hormones. Gastrin causes the secretion of gastric juice, while secretin and CCK cause the secretion of pancreatic juice.

◆ Carnivores such as dogs have teeth adapted to kill and tear prey. Herbivores such as cows have teeth adapted to grind grass and other plants, in order to begin the breakdown of cellulose cell walls. The rumen of a cow contains microorganisms which can digest cellulose.

Questions

1 Compare the structures of the wall of the stomach and ileum, and discuss how they are adapted for their functions.

2 Outline the roles of
 a the liver and
 b the pancreas
 in digestion in humans.

3 Distinguish between:
 a excretion and egestion;
 b endopeptidases and exopeptidases;
 c heterotrophs and autotrophs;
 d mechanical digestion and chemical digestion.

4 Describe how the digestive system of a cow differs from that of a human, and explain the functional significance of the differences you describe.

CHAPTER 2

The liver

By the end of this chapter you should be able to:

1 describe the gross structure of the liver, including its associated blood vessels;

2 describe the histology of the liver and recognise this using the light microscope;

3 explain the roles of the liver in carbohydrate metabolism and the production of glucose from amino acids;

4 explain the roles of the liver in fat metabolism, including the use of fats in respiration, the synthesis of triglycerides from excess carbohydrate and protein, the synthesis and regulation of cholesterol, and the transport of lipids to and from the liver as lipoproteins;

5 explain the roles of the liver in deamination, transamination and urea formation;

6 describe the production, and explain the roles, of the plasma proteins fibrinogen, globulins and albumin;

7 describe the production and use of bile;

8 outline the roles of the liver in detoxification;

9 describe the metabolism of alcohol in the liver, and the long-term consequences of excessive alcohol consumption.

The liver is one of the largest organs in the body. 29 % of the blood that is pumped with each heartbeat flows through the liver; a total of 1450 cm³ of blood passes through it in one minute. It has an enormous variety of functions involving many different metabolic reactions. Yet, even when seen under the microscope, its structure appears considerably more uniform than that of most other organs.

The structure of the liver

The liver lies just beneath the diaphragm (*figure 2.1*), towards the right-hand side of the body. It is made up of several lobes.

Blood supply

The blood supply to the liver is unlike that of any other organ in the body, because it arrives in two different blood vessels. The **hepatic artery** leads

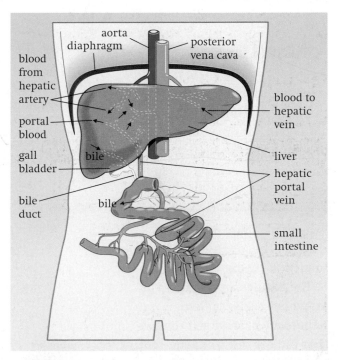

● **Figure 2.1** The structure of the liver and its associated organs.

from the aorta and delivers oxygenated blood to the liver. The **hepatic portal vein** leads from the small intestine and delivers blood rich in absorbed nutrients. The hepatic portal vein carries about three times as much blood to the liver each minute as the hepatic artery. The blood in the hepatic portal vein has already passed through a set of capillaries, in the wall of the small intestine, and so it is at a much lower pressure than the blood in the hepatic artery, and is deoxygenated. A single vessel, the **hepatic vein**, carries blood away from the liver to the vena cava, which then transports it back to the heart (*figure 2.2*).

SAQ 2.1

Suggest one other difference, apart from pressure and oxygen concentration, between the blood carried to the liver in the hepatic artery and that carried in the hepatic portal vein.

Histology of the liver

Figures 2.3 and *2.4* show the structure of liver tissue. It is made up of many **lobules**, up to 100 000 in a human. In the centre of each lobule is a branch of the hepatic vein. Between the lobules are branches of the hepatic artery and the hepatic portal vein. Blood flows from here, through the lobules, and into the branch of the hepatic vein.

The lobules are made up of many liver cells, called **hepatocytes**, arranged in rows that radiate out from the centre like spokes in a wheel. The channels which carry blood

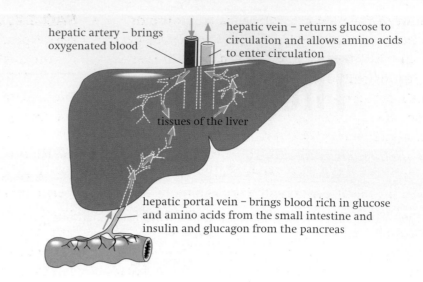

● **Figure 2.2** The blood supply of the liver.

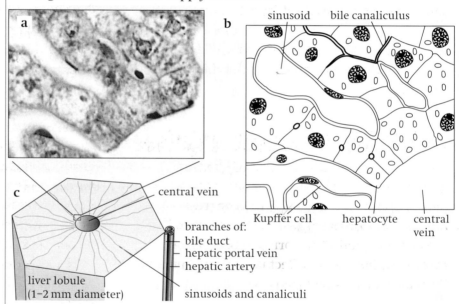

● **Figure 2.3** Histology of the liver. **a** Light micrograph (× 1000). **b** Diagram of the tissue shown in the micrograph. **c** The structure of a complete liver lobule.

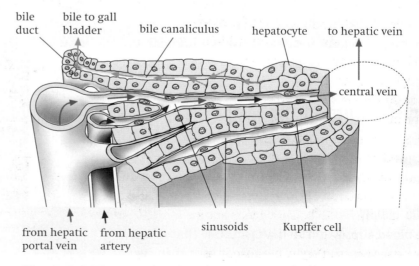

● **Figure 2.4** Diagram showing the structure of a liver lobule.

between these rows of cells are called **sinusoids**. Other channels carry **bile**, which is produced by some of the hepatocytes; these channels are called **bile canaliculi**. The bile flows from the centre of the lobule towards the outside (that is, in the opposite direction to the blood flow), where it enters a branch of the **bile duct**. The rows of hepatocytes are never more than two cells thick, so that each individual cell is in close contact with the blood in the sinusoids.

The sinusoids are lined with large, phagocytic macrophages (see *Biology 1*, page 221). The macrophages capture and destroy bacteria which enter the liver via the hepatic portal vein, in blood that has come from the intestine. These cells are sometimes known as **Kupffer cells**. They are very efficient at this; if a bacterium comes into contact with the plasma membrane of a Kupffer cell, it is taken into the cell by phagocytosis within 0.01 second.

Carbohydrate metabolism in the liver

The liver is involved in the control of blood glucose levels, working together with the pancreas and adrenal glands. The pancreas secretes the hormones **insulin** and **glucagon**, and the adrenal glands the hormone **adrenaline**, and these three hormones affect the way in which the liver cells metabolise carbohydrates.

Interconversion of glucose and glycogen

Carbohydrates are transported in human blood in the form of the monosaccharide **glucose**. Glucose is the main respiratory substrate for many tissues in the body. As it has small and soluble molecules, it is not suitable as a storage compound, and so if there is more glucose in the blood than is needed, some of it is converted into the polysaccharide **glycogen** and stored. The liver and muscles are the main storage organs for glycogen, with the liver containing around 25 % of these stores and the muscles 75 %. Glycogen granules can be seen in liver cells using a good light microscope; they can make up as much as 8 % of the total mass of the cell.

SAQ 2.2_____
What type of reaction will be involved in converting glucose to glycogen?

The control of blood glucose levels by insulin and glucagon is described in *Biology 2*, pages 101–6. When blood glucose levels fall, α cells in the islets of Langerhans secrete the hormone **glucagon**. Glucagon binds to glycoprotein receptors in the plasma membranes of hepatocytes, and this sets into action a series of events in the cytoplasm of the cell that results in the breakdown of glycogen into glucose. This process is called **glycogenolysis** ('lysis' means 'breaking down', so this word simply means 'breaking down glycogen'). The glucose passes out of the hepatocyte and into the blood, helping to raise blood glucose levels back towards normal (*figure 2.5*).

When blood glucose levels are high, β cells in the islets of Langerhans in the pancreas secrete **insulin** into the blood. Insulin acts on hepatocytes to stimulate them to convert glucose into glycogen. (Insulin also affects the behaviour of muscle cells and fat-containing cells in adipose tissue, increasing the rate at which they take up and metabolise glucose.) This helps to lower blood glucose levels towards normal.

The hormone **adrenaline**, released from the adrenal glands in times of stress, has a similar effect to that of glucagon. The breakdown of glycogen reserves to glucose provides extra fuel to muscles, which may need to work hard in order to escape or battle with the source of danger.

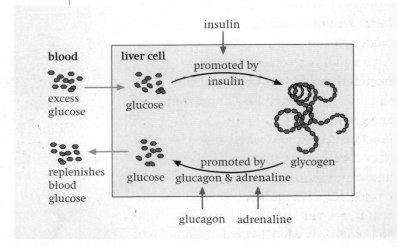

● **Figure 2.5** Carbohydrate metabolism in the liver.

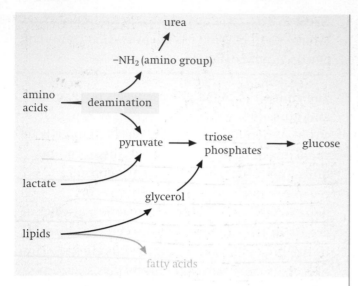

• **Figure 2.6** Gluconeogenesis in the liver.

Interconversion of other substances with carbohydrates

Besides converting glycogen to glucose and glucose to glycogen, the liver can also convert non-carbohydrate substances, including amino acids, fats, lactate and pyruvate, to glucose (*figure 2.6*). This is known as **gluconeogenesis**. ('Neo' means 'new', so 'gluco-neo-genesis' means 'making new glucose'.)

Gluconeogenesis happens in response to the hormone glucagon. In normal circumstances, gluconeogenesis only takes place when all supplies of glycogen have been exhausted, such as after more than 12 hours of fasting. When blood glucose levels are low and the liver has no glycogen left to draw upon, it begins to convert **amino acids** into glucose. The amino acids are first deaminated (described on pages 22–3). The nitrogen-containing part of the amino acid molecule is converted to urea, which will be excreted from the body through the kidneys. The rest of the molecule is converted first to **pyruvate** and then to glucose.

Lactate is produced when anaerobic respiration takes place in tissues, especially muscles (see *Biology 1*, pages 180–1, and *Biology 2*, page 12). Lactate is taken in by the hepatocytes, and converted first to pyruvate and then to glucose. **Glycerol**, from lipids, can also be converted to glucose.

All of the functions described above occur in response to *low* levels of glucose in the blood. When glucose levels are *high*, the liver converts some of it to fats, for storage. We will look at this in more detail in the next section.

Lipid metabolism

Lipids (fats) can be used to generate ATP by respiration. They are also very important as energy-storage compounds; they are stored in the cells that make up **adipose tissue**. Unlike carbohydrates, they also have structural roles in the body, as they are the main component of all cell membranes. Steroids, which are derived from lipids, form several different hormones. The liver plays a central role in all aspects of lipid metabolism (*figure 2.7*).

SAQ 2.3

From your knowledge of the structure and properties of lipid molecules, suggest why they make good energy–storage compounds.

Fats as an energy source

Fats can be used in respiration to form ATP. They are an important energy source in humans at all times, even when there is plenty of glucose in the blood. In fact, most tissues will use fatty acids

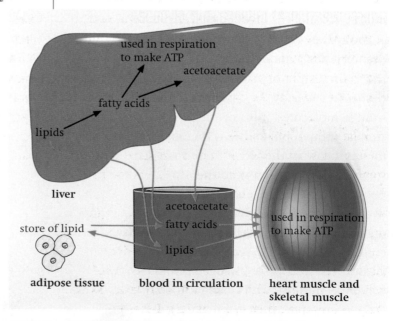

• **Figure 2.7** The role of the liver in lipid metabolism.

rather than glucose as their 'first choice' respiratory substrate; the only exceptions are nervous tissue and red blood cells, which must use glucose. Cardiac muscle, in particular, uses fatty acids rather than glucose as its respiratory substrate. And, if glucose is in short supply – perhaps because the person has not eaten for some time – then fats are increasingly used by other body tissues as well.

SAQ 2.4

a Explain why red blood cells cannot carry out aerobic respiration.

b Fatty acids are fed into the Krebs cycle when they are used in respiration. Explain why red blood cells are unable to use fatty acids as a respiratory substrate.

The liver can use fat as a respiratory substrate. Triglyceride molecules are first split into glycerol and fatty acids, inside the hepatocytes. The fatty acids are converted into acetyl coenzyme A, which can be fed into the Krebs cycle to produce ATP (*Biology 2*, page 8). Glycerol → Glucose

When the body is short of carbohydrate, for example if a person is fasting, then more and more fatty acids are broken down in the liver. The liver cells cannot use all of the acetyl coenzyme A that is formed, so they convert some of it into a substance called acetoacetate (a ketone) and then release it into the blood. Although the liver itself cannot use acetoacetate, many other tissues can, and they absorb it from the blood and convert it back to acetyl coenzyme A before feeding it into the Krebs cycle for the production of ATP.

Synthesis of triglycerides

The liver is responsible for the conversion of excess carbohydrate and protein to fat. Some of this fat is **triglyceride**. Once made, the triglycerides are transported to other parts of the body, where they are stored in adipose tissue.

As fats are insoluble in water, they cannot be transported just as they are. They are combined with protein molecules to form **lipoproteins**. Most triglycerides are transported as **low density lipoproteins** or **LDLs** (*figure 2.8*). A lipoprotein is a

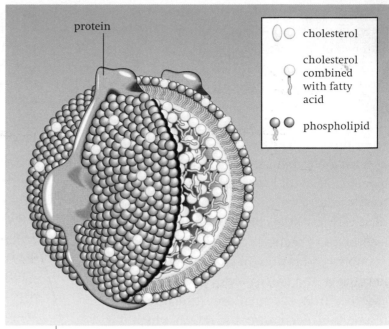

● **Figure 2.8** A low density lipoprotein (LDL).

particle made up of many lipid and protein molecules. The centre is filled with hydrophobic lipids, while the outside consists of a 'shell' of polar lipids and proteins. There are many types of lipoproteins which carry different types of fats from and to different parts of the body. They are named according to their relative densities.

Synthesis and regulation of cholesterol

The liver makes **cholesterol**. *Figure 2.9* shows the structure of a cholesterol molecule.

Cholesterol has a number of very important functions in the body. It is an essential component of cell membranes (*Biology 1*, pages 53–4), where it helps to maintain their mechanical stability, regulate their fluidity, and maintain their relative impermeability to hydrophilic substances. It is also needed for the synthesis of steroid hormones such as oestrogen and testosterone. It is deposited in the skin, which

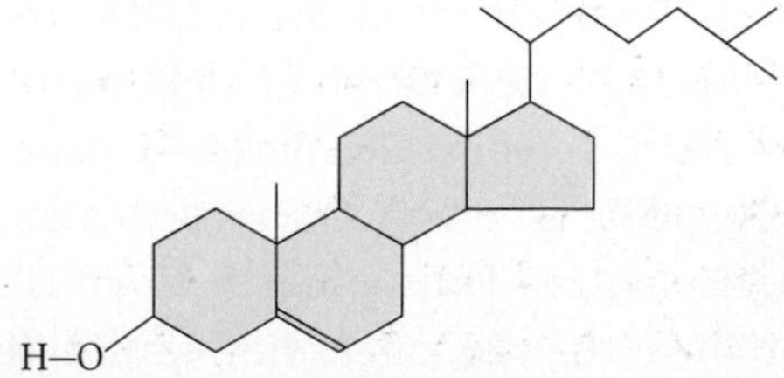

● **Figure 2.9** The structure of a cholesterol molecule.

it helps to waterproof, so preventing both loss of water by evaporation from the body and uptake of water-soluble substances from outside. Vitamin D is made from cholesterol, in skin cells stimulated by ultraviolet light. Cholesterol is also used for making bile salts (page 7).

Despite this, cholesterol has acquired a reputation for being very bad for you. It is present in most diets, and it is true that people with high blood cholesterol levels are more likely to suffer from cardiovascular disease than people with relatively low levels (*Biology 1*, pages 193–4). The liver helps to regulate these levels.

Cholesterol is present in the diet, especially in meat, eggs and dairy products. When it is absorbed from the small intestine, the liver responds by decreasing the rate at which it synthesises cholesterol. This happens because the dietary cholesterol reduces the activity of one of the enzymes that catalyses the synthesis of cholesterol from acetyl coenzyme A. Thus, dietary cholesterol does not always have a significant effect on the levels of cholesterol in the blood. On the other hand, large quantities of saturated fats (that is, fats containing no carbon–carbon double bonds) in the diet do cause the liver to increase the rate at which it converts these to cholesterol. For this reason, it is usually recommended that people keep the amount of saturated fat in their diet to a relatively low level. There is, however, growing evidence that for many people genotype has an even greater effect on their cardiovascular health than their diet does.

Cholesterol is not water-soluble, and so is transported – like triglycerides – in the blood plasma as lipoproteins. Some is transported as low density or very low density lipoproteins, and some as high density lipoproteins, **HDLs**. The relative proportion of LDLs and HDLs in the blood appears to have far more of an effect on health than the actual quantities of either of these. LDLs are associated with the deposition of cholesterol as plaques on blood vessel walls (*Biology 1*, page 194), while HDLs appear to protect against this and may even remove plaques. Thus a high ratio of HDLs to LDLs can reduce the risk of cardiovascular disease.

Protein metabolism

The liver is responsible for many aspects of protein metabolism. It is in the hepatocytes that the conversion of one type of amino acid to another, and also the deamination of excess amino acids and the production of urea takes place. The liver also makes many different proteins, including the important blood proteins fibrinogen, albumin and globulins.

Transamination

Transamination is the conversion of one amino acid to another (*figure 2.10*). There are 20 different amino acids that are used to build proteins. If the mix that we have eaten in our food does not match the body's requirements, then the liver is able to convert a type of amino acid that is in ample supply in our cells into another kind which is not present in sufficiently large amounts.

However, not all amino acids can be formed in this way. Some, which are known as **essential amino acids**, can only be obtained from our diet. These are listed in *Table 12.5* on page 162 in *Biology 1*.

Deamination and the formation of urea

The human body is not able to store excess amino acids. If we eat more than we require, then the excess must somehow be dealt with.

The liver cells are able to turn these excess amino acids into useful substances such as carbohydrates (described on page 20) and fats. This involves the removal of the nitrogen-containing

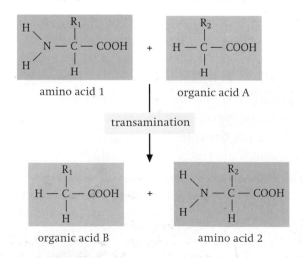

● **Figure 2.10** Transamination.

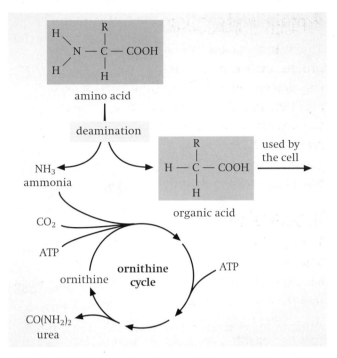

● **Figure 2.11** Deamination and the ornithine cycle.

part of the molecule, the amine group. The removal of the amine group from an amino acid is called **deamination** (*figure 2.11*).

The carbon-containing product of this reaction can, as we have seen, be converted into carbohydrate or fat, which can be respired or stored. The nitrogen-containing part is **ammonia**, which is highly toxic and highly soluble. With input of energy from ATP, the ammonia is combined with carbon dioxide to form **urea**, in a series of steps involving the successive formation of several amino acids, which is known as the **ornithine cycle**. A human eating an average amount of protein in their diet will produce around 25–30 g of urea each day. The urea is

released from the hepatocytes into the blood, and is excreted by the kidneys (*Biology 2*, pages 89–97).

SAQ 2.5

Animals that live in water, such as fish, often excrete their nitrogenous waste in the form of ammonia, rather than as urea.

a Explain why it is possible for them to do this, whereas terrestrial animals cannot.

b Suggest the advantages to aquatic animals of excreting ammonia rather than urea.

Synthesis of plasma proteins

The blood contains many different kinds of proteins dissolved in the plasma, all of which – as would be expected of a soluble protein – are globular. They are known as **plasma proteins**. They include fibrinogen, globulin and albumin. Almost all of the plasma proteins, except for immunoglobulins (antibodies) are made in the liver.

Fibrinogen and **prothrombin** are important in blood clotting (*figure 2.12*). They are both globular, soluble proteins. When a blood vessel is damaged, collagen fibres in its walls are exposed. This activates platelets (tiny cell fragments in the blood), and also sets into action a cascade of events that results in the conversion of prothrombin to an active enzyme called **thrombin**. Thrombin catalyses the removal of some amino acids from fibrinogen molecules, converting the fibrinogen to a form in which many molecules can link together (polymerise) in a long chain to form **fibrin**. Fibrin is insoluble, and it forms fibres that tangle up with each other

a

exposure of blood to collagen e.g. in a wound → prothrombin

fibrinogen

thrombin →

fibrin

Fibrin forms insoluble fibres that trap red cells.

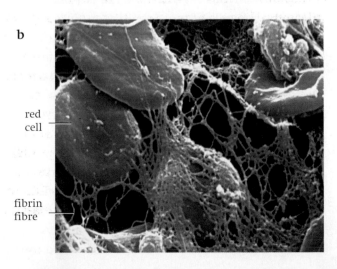

red cell

fibrin fibre

● **Figure 2.12 a** The roles of fibrinogen and prothrombin in blood clotting. **b** Scanning e.m. of part of a blood clot (× 3000). The tangled threads in which the red blood cells are trapped are fibrin fibres.

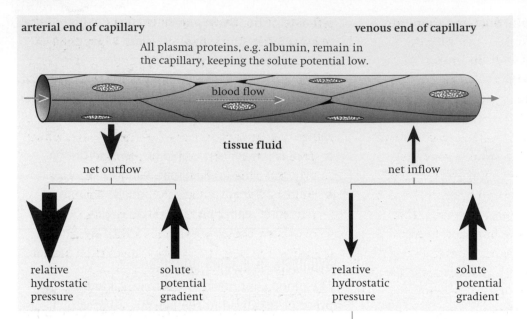

arterial end of capillary

venous end of capillary

All plasma proteins, e.g. albumin, remain in the capillary, keeping the solute potential low.

blood flow

tissue fluid

net outflow

net inflow

relative hydrostatic pressure

solute potential gradient

relative hydrostatic pressure

solute potential gradient

● **Figure 2.13** The role of plasma proteins in the formation and reabsorption of tissue fluid.

to form a mesh in which platelets and red blood cells get trapped. This not only stops blood from escaping from the wound, but also prevents the entry of pathogens from outside.

Globulin is a term used for most of the globular proteins in blood plasma. Some of these are antibodies (immunoglobulins), and these are *not* made by the liver but by cells of the immune system (*Biology 1*, pages 220–6). The other globulins are made by the liver. Many of them help to transport other molecules, such as the hormone thyroxine, insulin and lipids, by combining with them in the blood plasma.

Albumin is the most abundant plasma protein. Its main function is to prevent too much water from leaving the blood in the tissues.

Albumin molecules are too large to pass through the walls of most capillaries (*Biology 1*, page 110). As blood passes through a capillary, water and many solute molecules are able to pass through tiny holes in the capillary walls and into the spaces between the cells making up the tissues, thus forming **tissue fluid** (*figure 2.13*).

The rate at which this happens depends on the relative magnitudes of two opposing tendencies. The first depends on the **relative hydrostatic pressure** in the capillary and in the tissue fluid – the former is always larger than the latter. Thus, the difference in hydrostatic pressure always tends to push water out of the capillary and into the tissue fluid. The second depends on the **solute potential gradient** between the blood and the tissue fluid. The presence of albumin molecules in the blood plasma, but not in the tissue fluid, means that the solute potential of the blood plasma is always lower than that of the tissue fluid.

The solute potential gradient therefore tends to make water move from the tissue fluid and into the blood, while the hydrostatic pressure gradient tends to make it move the other way.

At the arterial end of the capillary, the hydrostatic pressure of the blood is relatively high, so the hydrostatic gradient is larger than the solute potential gradient, so fluid flows from the blood and into the tissue fluid. However, at the venous end, much water has been lost from the blood, so its hydrostatic pressure is lower. The hydrostatic gradient is therefore smaller than the solute potential gradient, so water flows back into the blood from the tissue fluid.

If it were not for the presence of albumin in the blood, the solute potential gradient would not be large enough to outweigh the hydrostatic pressure gradient, even at the venous end of the capillary. Water would accumulate in the tissue fluid, and not return to the blood. The tissues would swell, a condition known as **oedema**. This explains the swollen belly of a child suffering from the protein deficiency disease **kwashiorkor** (*Biology 1*, page 166). There is not enough albumin in the blood to help fluid drain back into the capillaries from the tissues.

The production of bile

Most of the cholesterol formed in the liver is used to make **bile**. In a human, about 1000 cm^3 of bile are made each day. Bile is made by the hepatocytes and secreted into the bile canaliculi. These carry some of the bile into the **bile duct** and then into the duodenum. Some is carried into the **gall bladder**, where it is stored and concentrated before being released into the bile duct.

Apart from water, the major component of bile is **bile salts**. These are made from cholesterol. As we have seen (page 7), they act like detergents and emulsify fats in the small intestine, making it easier for them to be digested by lipase and to be absorbed into the lymphatic capillaries in the villi.

Bile also contains cholesterol. Normally, this cholesterol interacts with the bile salts to form water-soluble particles, but sometimes (for example, if there is too much cholesterol in the bile, or too little water or bile salts) it may precipitate out and form gallstones (*figure 2.14*). Sometimes, gallstones may contain calcium deposits as well as cholesterol. The gallstones may remain in the gall bladder, or get into the bile duct and block it. They can be very painful and may prevent bile from flowing into the duodenum, so interfering with digestion of fats. Gallstones can be removed by surgery, or by ultrasound treatment which breaks them into many tiny pieces that can flow away in the bile. Gallstones containing only cholesterol can be dissolved away by giving the patient extra bile acids over a period of a few years.

Bile also contains breakdown products from red blood cells. A red blood cell is short-lived, rarely surviving much more than 120 days. Old red blood cells are broken down in the spleen (a soft organ that lies just below the diaphragm on the left side of the body) and in the liver. Some of the haemoglobin from these cells is broken down in several parts of the body, including the liver, into haem and globin. The globin part of the molecule is then hydrolysed to individual amino acids, which can be used in protein synthesis. The haem group is split into an iron-containing part, which is stored in the liver, and a greenish-yellow compound called **bilirubin**. The liver secretes bilirubin into bile, where it has no known function – it is simply an excretory product.

New-born babies sometimes suffer from jaundice, in which their blood gives their skin a decidedly yellow appearance. This happens because a very young baby, especially if it is pre-mature, may not yet have liver cells that are capable of dealing with bilirubin and excreting it into the bile. So bilirubin accumulates in the blood. Exposure to ultraviolet light causes the bilirubin in the blood to break down, and this is often used to help babies suffering from jaundice.

Detoxification

Many potentially dangerous substances that find their way into the body are broken down by the liver. Some of them may be broken down into different, harmless substances, while some may be excreted into the bile. Most of these processes take place on the smooth endoplasmic reticulum in the hepatocytes.

Metabolism of alcohol

Alcoholic drinks contain **ethanol**, C_2H_5OH. Ethanol molecules are small and lipid-soluble, so they very easily diffuse across plasma membranes and enter cells. Ethanol is a toxic substance, and can cause considerable damage to cells. The liver helps to avoid such damage by breaking down ethanol into harmless substances.

The enzyme that catalyses the breakdown of ethanol is **alcohol dehydrogenase** (*figure 2.15 overleaf*). Ethanol is first converted to ethanal (acetaldehyde) by this enzyme, and then to ethanoate (acetate) by **aldehyde dehydrogenase**. This can enter the Krebs cycle and be metabolised to produce ATP. Ethanol is therefore a source of energy for cells, its oxidation providing $30\,kJ\,g^{-1}$.

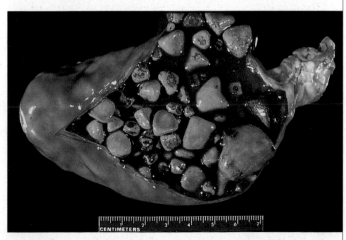

● **Figure 2.14** A human gall bladder which has been removed by surgery, cut open to show the gallstones it contains.

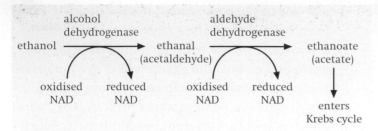

● **Figure 2.15** Detoxification of alcohol in the liver.

If large quantities of alcohol are consumed on a regular basis, then the tissues within the liver can be damaged. You can see, in *figure 2.15*, that the breakdown of ethanol produces reduced NAD. This means that reactions needing *oxidised* NAD are less likely to take place. These include the oxidation of fatty acids (page 21). So fatty acids accumulate, and are converted to fats, which are deposited in the liver. The amount of fat in the liver appears to be correlated with the amount of alcohol consumed, rather than any other aspect of the diet. The fat is stored in the hepatocytes, and can severely reduce their efficiency at carrying out many of the other functions of the liver. Such a condition is known as **fatty liver**.

A combination of these effects, plus the direct toxic effects on the liver cells caused by ethanol, leads to a condition known as **cirrhosis** of the liver. Liver cells are destroyed by the ethanol. They are replaced, but the normal structure of the lobules is lost, and large amounts of fibrous tissue are laid down (*figure 2.16*). The structure of the blood supply is also lost, so that some blood that arrives via the hepatic portal vein simply goes straight past and into the hepatic vein, without flowing through the sinusoids on the way. There are causes of cirrhosis of the liver other than the intake of alcohol, but many people with this condition are chronic alcoholics.

A liver that is affected by cirrhosis cannot carry out its normal functions effectively. Because there are so many of these, a very wide variety of damaging effects are seen in someone with cirrhosis of the liver. For example, the liver cells can no longer convert ammonia (from the deamination of amino acids) to urea as efficiently as normal. So ammonia accumulates in the blood and can cause considerable damage to the central nervous sytem. In severe cases, coma and even death may ensue.

Breakdown of other substances

The liver breaks down many hormones that are produced within the body. Although these are not toxic, it is important that they do not remain in the blood for too long, or else the effects that they cause would go on and on for ever. Examples of hormones broken down in the liver include thyroxine, oestrogen and testosterone. Liver damage can therefore lead to the accumulation of one or more hormones in the body, which in turn may cause disruption to processes that are affected by these hormones.

Drugs taken for medicinal reasons, such as antibiotics, barbiturates and paracetamol, are broken down in the liver. Once again, it is important that such drugs should be eliminated from the body after a short while.

The elimination of the breakdown products of hormones or drugs (and also some unchanged hormones) from the body is done via the kidneys. You will remember that, after filtration in a Bowman's capsule, fluid flows along a nephron. Any lipid-soluble substances in this fluid can easily pass through the plasma membranes of the cells lining the nephrons and return to the blood. Water-soluble substances, however, tend to remain in the fluid inside the nephron, so that they are carried into the bladder in the urine and then lost to the outside. The liver helps this to occur because, as it breaks down hormones and drugs, it converts lipid-soluble molecules, such as steroids, to water-soluble ones.

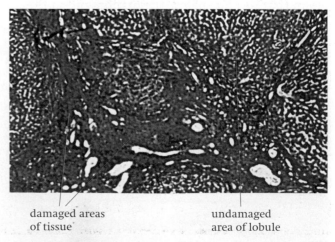

damaged areas of tissue   undamaged area of lobule

● **Figure 2.16** Light micrograph of liver tissue (× 35) showing cirrhosis. The fibrous tissue is stained a slightly darker pink than the normal parts of the lobules.

SUMMARY

◆ The liver is supplied with blood through the hepatic artery and the hepatic portal vein. Blood is taken away from the liver in the hepatic vein.

◆ The liver is made up of many lobules, in which liver cells called hepatocytes are arranged in rows radiating from the centre of each lobule. There is a branch of the hepatic vein at the centre of each lobule, and branches of the hepatic artery and hepatic portal vein in the spaces between lobules. Sinusoids carry blood between the hepatocytes, while bile canaliculi carry bile.

◆ The liver interconverts glucose and glycogen, which helps to maintain a constant level of glucose in the blood. The hormones adrenaline and glucagon increase the rate at which glycogen is converted to glucose (glycogenolysis) whereas insulin increases the rate at which glucose is converted to glycogen.

◆ Other substances, especially amino acids, are converted to glucose in the liver. This is known as gluconeogenesis.

◆ Liver cells can use fatty acids as an energy source. They also convert fatty acids to acetoacetate (ketone) which is released into the blood and used by other cells as a respiratory substrate.

◆ Liver cells produce lipids from carbohydrates and proteins.

◆ Lipids are transported in the blood as lipoproteins, small spheres made up of fat and protein.

◆ Cholesterol is made in the liver, and the rate at which this happens is reduced if the diet contains large amounts of cholesterol.

◆ Cholesterol is transported in the blood as low density and high density lipoproteins. A high ratio of high density lipoproteins to low density lipoproteins may lower the risk of cardiovascular disease.

◆ Transamination, the conversion of one amino acid to another, occurs in the liver. Some amino acids, known as essential amino acids, cannot be made in this way.

◆ Excess amino acids are deaminated in the liver, and the amine group is converted first to ammonia and then to urea via the ornithine cycle.

◆ The liver synthesises the plasma proteins fibrinogen, globulins (apart from immunoglobulins) and albumin. Fibrinogen is essential for blood clotting. Globulins help to transport various substances in the blood plasma. Albumin maintains the low solute potential of the blood, which helps water to return to the blood from tissue fluid.

◆ Bile is made in the liver and stored in the gall bladder. It contains bile salts, which emulsify fats in the small intestine, and also bilirubin, which is an excretory product resulting from the breakdown of haemoglobin.

◆ Many hormones, drugs and toxic substances are broken down in the liver. The breakdown of ethanol results in the formation of excess amounts of reduced NAD, and this can inhibit the oxidation of fatty acids. Fats therefore accumulate in the livers of people who regularly drink large quantities of alcohol. Further damage can result in liver cirrhosis.

Questions

1 Discuss the role of the liver in homeostasis.

2 Discuss the ways in which the structure of the liver is related to its functions.

3 Hepatitis is a disease of the liver, caused by pathogenic viruses which damage liver cells. Suggest how damage to the liver may produce each of the following symptoms of hepatitis:
   a poor digestion of fats;
   b jaundice;
   c poor blood clotting.

4 Describe the roles of the liver in:
   a fat metabolism;
   b protein metabolism.

CHAPTER 3

Support and locomotion

By the end of this chapter you should be able to:

1 use the light microscope to interpret the structure of compact bone and hyaline cartilage;

2 relate the structure of a thoracic and a lumbar vertebra to their functions;

3 identify the major limb bones of a mammal;

4 describe the structure of a synovial joint and identify the different types of joint;

5 describe the lever action of the human arm, and explain how antagonistic muscles work together to produce movement;

6 describe the histology and ultrastructure of striated muscle;

7 describe the sliding filament theory of muscle contraction, including the roles of troponin and tropomyosin;

8 describe the structure of a neuromuscular junction and explain how a nerve impulse causes muscle to contract;

9 outline the effects of ageing on the locomotory system with reference to osteoarthritis and osteoporosis.

The human skeleton, like that of all mammals, is a structure made from relatively hard materials – bone and cartilage – that supports the body. It acts as a solid framework to which muscles are attached, allowing the forces produced by muscle contraction to be transmitted to the body in such a way that movement is produced. Some parts of the skeleton also help to protect vulnerable internal organs, such as the lungs, heart and brain.

A skeleton such as this, situated inside the body with soft tissues on the outside of it, is known as an **endoskeleton**. In contrast, arthropods such as insects have an **exoskeleton**, in which the hard, supportive materials are on the outside of the body, with all the soft tissues beneath them. Although the protective function of an endoskeleton may not be as great as that of an exoskeleton, endoskeletons are better able to support a large body, and this has enabled mammals and other vertebrates to grow to a much larger size than any arthropods will ever be able to do.

In this chapter, we will first consider the structure of the human skeleton, and then consider how the skeleton and muscles work together to produce movement. We will also look briefly at some of the changes that take place in the locomotory system as a person grows older.

The structure of the human skeleton

Figure 3.1 overleaf shows the structure of the human skeleton. The majority of it is made of a hard, relatively incompressible tissue called **bone**. Some parts, however, are made of a more flexible material called **cartilage**. As a fetus develops, the skeleton is first laid down as cartilage, most of which is gradually replaced by bone during growth and development. This process is called **ossification**. By the time that the baby is born, most bones are completely ossified except for an area near their ends. The cartilage here allows the bones to grow as the child grows. Cartilage remains throughout life as a covering over the ends of bones at moveable joints, for reasons which we will see later, and in some parts of the skeleton which need to be flexible, such as the ends of the ribs.

Before we look at the structure and functions of the different parts of the skeleton, it is useful to consider the histology and properties of the two materials from which it is made.

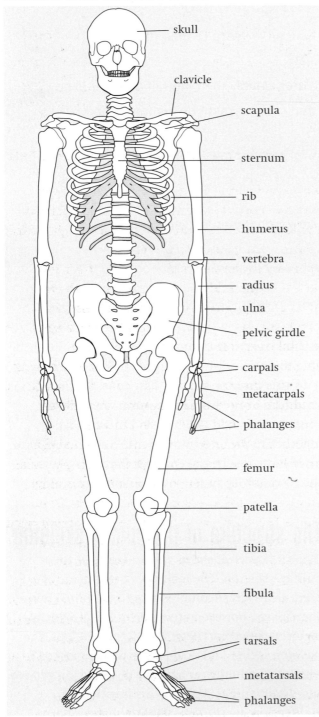

● **Figure 3.1** The human skeleton.

The histology of bone and cartilage

Both bone and cartilage are living tissues. They contain living cells, which are supplied with nutrients and oxygen by the blood system in the same way as any cells.

The structure of bone

Figure 3.2a is a micrograph of a transverse section through a bone. This type of bone is known as **compact bone**, in contrast to a more open-textured tissue called spongy bone that is found, for example, near the ends of the limb bones (*figure 3.3*, overleaf). Compact bone makes up the outer layers of the shafts of the long bones in the

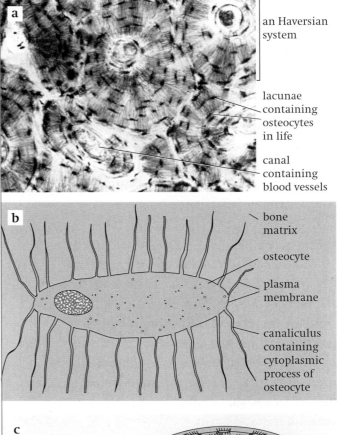

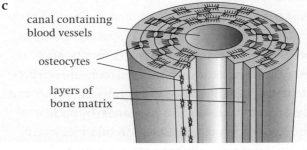

● **Figure 3.2** The structure of compact bone.
a Light micrograph of a transverse section of compact bone (× 55).   **b** An osteocyte.
c 3D structure of an Haversian system.

limbs, and also the outer parts of flat bones such as the ribs.

The most striking feature of compact bone, when seen under the microscope, is the close packing of many concentric circular arrangements. Each circle, with its concentric layers, is a **Haversian system**. You should try to imagine these in three dimensions – the circles are really cylinders, extending lengthways for about 5 mm.

In most prepared slides of bone that you will see through the microscope, you will be looking at a ground section of bone – as you can imagine, it is not easy to cut thin sections in the same way as you could, say, from a piece of stomach wall. In the process of preparing a ground section, the living bone cells are lost. In life, each of the dark spaces that you can see on the micrograph – the **lacunae** – and the thread-like **canaliculi** which branch from them, are filled with these living cells known as **osteocytes**.

Osteocytes began their life as bone-forming cells called **osteoblasts**. These cells synthesise and secrete the fibrous protein **tropocollagen**, which is deposited outside their plasma membranes. Here the tropocollagen molecules link up with each other end-to-end and side-to-side to form **collagen** fibres (see *Biology 1*, page 36). Amongst these collagen fibres, an inorganic mineral consisting largely of **calcium phosphate** is deposited. This mineral also contains small amounts of magnesium and carbonate ions. Thus the cells become totally surrounded by, and trapped within, a **matrix** made of a mixture of organic materials (mostly collagen) and inorganic ones (mostly calcium phosphate). The organic material makes up about 30 % by weight of bone, while the inorganic matrix makes up 60 % and the osteocytes the remaining 10 %.

Bone is therefore a composite material, with a matrix containing different components with different properties. The organic component gives bone considerable **tensile strength** – that is, it can withstand very strong *pulling* forces (*figure 3.3*). This results from the presence of collagen fibres, which are intrinsically very strong but can be stretched enough to allow a bone to 'give' a little. The inorganic component provides bone with rigidity and **compressive strength** – that is, it can

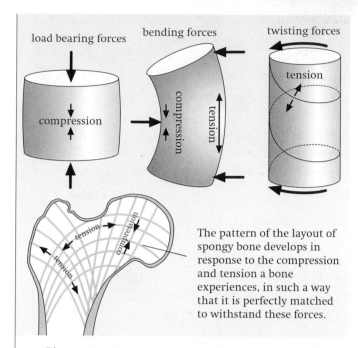

The pattern of the layout of spongy bone develops in response to the compression and tension a bone experiences, in such a way that it is perfectly matched to withstand these forces.

● **Figure 3.3** Forces acting on bones, and their effects.

withstand strong forces *pushing* on it. You can imagine how important this is in bones such as the leg bones, which have the whole weight of the body pressing down onto them.

The osteocytes, imprisoned within their own secretory material, maintain contact with each other through their cytoplasmic processes in the canaliculi. In the centre of each Haversian system is a canal containing an artery, a vein and a lymphatic vessel, which supply the osteocytes with nutrients and oxygen and take away their waste products. The canal also contains nerve fibres.

So, bone is laid down by osteoblasts and maintained by osteocytes (which were, in their early life, osteoblasts). Perhaps surprisingly, living bone is also continually being broken down by another group of cells called **osteoclasts**. This allows the structure of a bone to be altered if need be, for example to respond to new stresses put onto it if its owner takes up a new form of exercise, or to repair damage. Normally, a balance is maintained between the activities of osteoclasts and osteoblasts, so that a continual programme of repair and replacement of bone takes place throughout life. However, in old age the activity of osteoclasts tends to be greater than that of osteoblasts, and this can lead to the condition known as **osteoporosis**. We will look at this in greater detail on page 44.

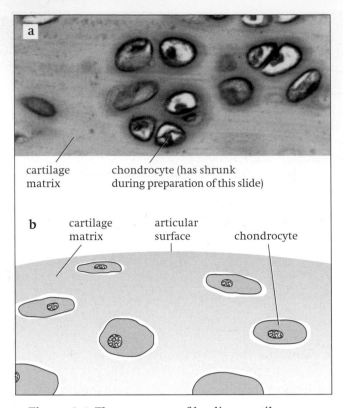

- **Figure 3.4** The structure of hyaline cartilage.
  a Light micrograph of hyaline cartilage (× 750).
  b Hyaline cartilage at the surface of a joint.

The structure of cartilage

Figure 3.4a is a micrograph of a transverse section through a kind of cartilage known as **hyaline cartilage**. 'Hyaline' comes from a Greek word meaning 'glass', and refers to the translucency of this tissue. Hyaline cartilage is found covering the ends of bones at moveable joints, in the ribs where they join to the sternum, and in the C-shaped cartilage rings that surround and support the trachea.

SAQ 3.1

Suggest why it is important that the ends of the ribs, where they join the sternum, are made of cartilage.

The living cells in cartilage are called **chondrocytes**. These cells are responsible for producing and maintaining the matrix in which they lie. Like all protein-secreting cells, chondrocytes have well-developed endoplasmic reticulum and Golgi apparatus. Unlike bone, this matrix does not normally contain calcium phosphate. It is a kind of water gel, made up of 75 % water and 25 % collagen and glycoproteins, which are secreted by the

chondrocytes. Another difference between cartilage and bone is that cartilage does not contain blood vessels, so the chondrocytes obtain their nutrients by diffusion from surrounding tissue fluids. Chondrocytes rely mainly on glycolysis to supply their ATP, so do not need a good oxygen supply.

Hyaline cartilage is a much more flexible material than bone, although it is still sufficiently rigid to provide support. At joints, the surface of the hyaline cartilage covering the ends of the bones is extremely smooth and slippery. This slipperiness is achieved by a thin layer of cartilage in which fine collagen fibres are closely packed and arranged parallel to the surface, and which is covered with a thin, very smooth, glycoprotein-rich layer.

Like bone, cartilage is continually broken down and renewed throughout life. As a person ages, the rate of breaking down tends to become greater than the rate of rebuilding, so some loss of cartilage can occur. When this happens at joints, **osteoarthritis** can result. This is described on page 44.

The axial skeleton

The axial skeleton comprises the bones aligned along the midline of the skeleton – that is the skull, vertebral column, ribs and sternum. Here we will concentrate only on the vertebral column.

Figure 3.5 shows the structure of the vertebral column of a human. It is made up of 33 **vertebrae**. There are 7 **cervical vertebrae** which support the head and neck; 12 **thoracic vertebrae** supporting the chest and articulating with the ribs; 5 **lumbar vertebrae** to which the large muscles of the lower back are attached; 5 fused **sacral vertebrae**, which together form the sacrum which articulates with and supports the hip bones; and 4 little 'tail' vertebrae, fused together to form the **coccyx**.

Figure 3.6a shows the structure of one vertebra from the lumbar region. The main load-bearing part is the **centrum**. Alongside this is the **neural arch**, beneath which the spinal cord lies, in life, in the **neural canal**.

Projecting outwards and sideways from the neural arch are bony processes to which muscles are attached. The ones to the side are **transverse processes** and the single backwardly-pointing one in the centre is the **neural spine**. Four smaller

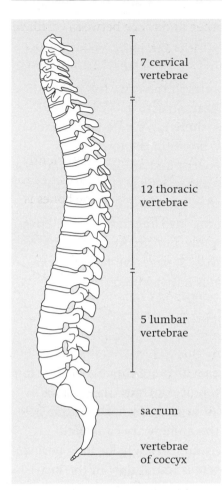

● **Figure 3.5** The vertebral column.

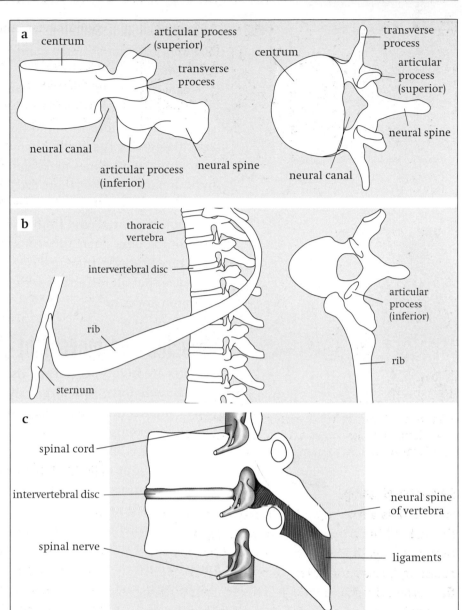

processes on the upper (that is, nearer the neck) and lower surfaces make contact with the vertebrae on either side. These are the **articular processes**.

The lumbar vertebrae are the most solid of all the vertebrae. You can see that, compared with the thoracic vertebra in *figure 3.6b*, they have a relatively large centrum, and large and substantial transverse processes. These are needed because the powerful muscles of the lower back are attached here. The neural spine is shorter and sturdier than in the thoracic vertebra.

Thoracic vertebrae articulate with the ribs, at the ends of the transverse processes and also at a point just above the centrum. The neural spines are much longer than in a lumbar vertebra, and they slope downwards (see side view).

A place where two bones meet is a **joint**, and the joints between the vertebrae are known as **intervertebral joints**. Each vertebra is joined to the next by **ligaments** (*figure 3.6c*). Between each

● **Figure 3.6** The structure of vertebrae. The bones on the right in diagrams **a** and **b** are drawn as though you were looking down onto a person's spine from above – that is, from the position of their head. The person's back is towards the right of the diagrams. **a** A lumbar vertebra. **b** Thoracic vertebrae. **c** How vertebrae articulate with each other.

vertebra and the ones on either side of it, there are discs of cartilage, **intervertebral discs**, which act as shock-absorbers. A relatively small amount of movement is possible at each intervertebral joint, but as there are many of them the total flexibility of the whole vertebral column is high.

Between each pair of vertebrae there is a small gap through which the spinal nerves emerge. Blood vessels also pass through these gaps.

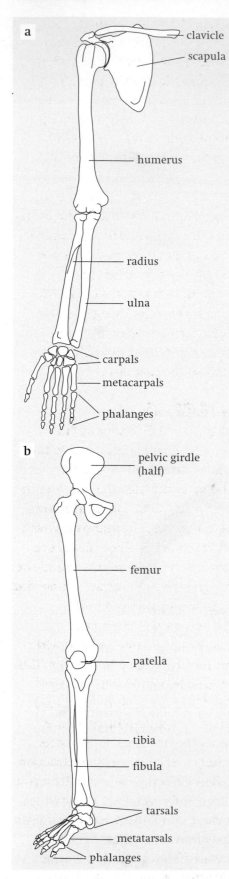

- **Figure 3.7** The appendicular skeleton. **a** Bones of the pectoral girdle and arm. **b** Bones of the pelvic girdle and leg.

The appendicular skeleton

The appendicular skeleton comprises the limb bones, the pectoral girdle and the pelvic girdle.

Figure 3.7 shows the major limb bones in the arm, leg and girdles of a human. You can see that their basic structure is extremely similar. In both fore and hind limbs, there is a single bone which articulates with the girdle, then two bones in the lower limb. Numerous small bones make up the wrist and ankle, hand and foot. In both hand and foot there are five digits. This basic structure is found in all living amphibians, reptiles, birds and mammals. It is known as a **pentadactyl limb**, meaning 'five-fingered'. The relative sizes of the bones may vary considerably, but the fundamental structure is always the same (see *Biology 2*, page 79). This is strong evidence that all terrestrial vertebrates have evolved from a common ancestor.

Muscles and movement

Muscles are highly specialised tissues which are capable of exerting considerable forces when they shorten or **contract**. The human body contains three different types of muscle. **Smooth muscle** is found, for example, in the walls of the alimentary canal and arterioles; it is able to contract slowly and strongly for long periods of time without tiring. **Cardiac muscle** is found only in the heart, where it contracts and relaxes rhythmically throughout life. The type of muscle attached to the skeleton, and which is responsible for all movements that are under conscious control, such as movement of the limbs and breathing movements, is **skeletal muscle**. Both cardiac and skeletal muscle appear stripey under the microscope, and so are both said to be **striated muscle**.

The structure of a joint

We have seen that, where two bones meet, a joint is formed. Sometimes, joints allow no movement at all, for example between the bones that make up the cranium. Sometimes, a small degree of movement is allowed, such as at the joints between the vertebrae. In other cases, much freer movement is possible.

The joints in the human body which allow the greatest degree of movement are in the limbs. At the joint between the humerus and the pectoral girdle, and also between the femur and pelvic girdle, a ball on the limb bone fits into a socket on the girdle. These are examples of **ball-and-socket joints**, and they allow a rotary movement (*figure 3.8a*). However, at the elbow and knee joints, the allowable movement is in one plane only, and these are examples of **hinge joints** (*figure 3.8b*).

SAQ 3.2

Give some other examples of hinge joints in the human body.

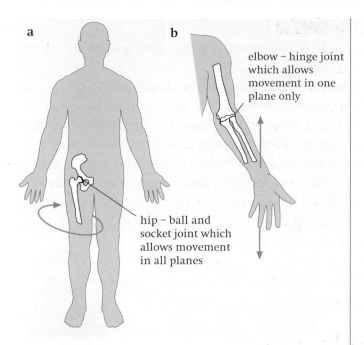

a

b

elbow – hinge joint
which allows
movement in one
plane only

hip – ball and
socket joint which
allows movement
in all planes

● **Figure 3.8** Types of movement at synovial joints.
a Ball-and-socket joint.   **b** Hinge joint.

Joints such as ball-and-socket and hinge joints, at which the two bones are able to move substantially with respect to each other, are known as **synovial joints**. The structure of a synovial hinge joint is shown in *figure 3.9*. The bones are held together by a **capsule** made of strong connective tissue containing collagen. This capsule may contain **ligaments**, and there are usually more ligaments either outside or inside the capsule. Ligaments are very tough strands of tissue made up mostly of collagen, and so they have high tensile strength.

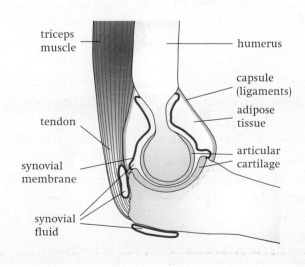

triceps
muscle

humerus

capsule
(ligaments)

adipose
tissue

tendon

articular
cartilage

synovial
membrane

synovial
fluid

● **Figure 3.9** The structure of the elbow joint.

The capsule is lined by a thin **synovial membrane**. The cells in the synovial membrane secrete small quantities of a clear, viscous fluid which fills all the spaces inside the capsule. The fluid helps to reduce friction between the ends of the bones. These cells also scavenge any foreign material in the joint cavity, such as pieces of cartilage that may have worn off the ends of the bones.

We saw earlier (page 32) that the ends of the bones at a synovial joint are covered with a thin, exceptionally smooth, layer of hyaline cartilage. This is called **articular cartilage** and, together with the synovial fluid, it allows an almost friction-free movement between the bones. The synovial fluid also provides the living chondrocytes in the cartilage with all their nutrients, which pass to the cells by diffusion through the matrix of the cartilage.

Movement at the elbow joint

Movement at joints is brought about by the **contraction** of muscles that are attached to the bones on either side of the joint. *Figure 3.10* overleaf shows the main muscles that are responsible for movement at the elbow joint. The muscles are attached to the bones by **tendons**, which are made from collagen fibres. These fibres run right into the bone at one end, and the muscle at the other, making an extremely strong connection through which the forces produced in the muscles can be transmitted to the bones.

Muscle tissue is made up of **fibres**, which are large, multinucleated cells. (The detailed structure of muscle is described on pages 37–40.) These fibres are able to use energy from ATP to exert a pulling force on the bones to which the muscle is attached. A muscle can only exert a force by contraction, not by lengthening. So there is usually a pair of muscles attached across a joint, arranged so that one can pull in one direction, and the other in the opposite direction. A pair of muscles arranged like this are said to be **antagonistic** muscles.

The elbow joint has, in fact, more than two muscles that cause its movement. The **biceps** muscle is attached to the scapula and

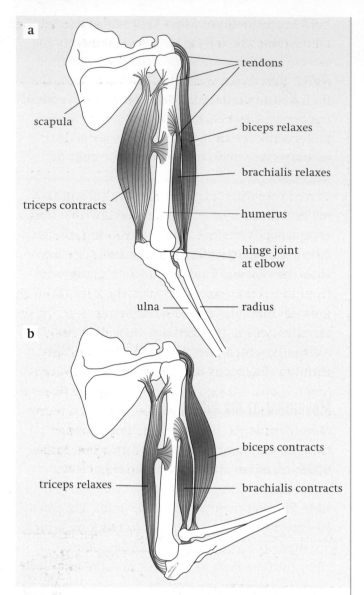

● **Figure 3.10** Movement at the elbow joint.
a Contraction of the triceps muscle lowers the arm (extension). **b** Contraction of the biceps and brachialis muscles raises the lower arm (flexion).

the radius, so that when it contracts it pulls the radius towards the scapula and the elbow joint bends. The **brachialis** muscle is attached to the humerus and the ulna, and has a similiar effect to the biceps when it contracts. Both of these muscles cause the elbow joint to bend or flex, and so they are **flexor** muscles.

The main muscle that is antagonistic to the biceps and brachialis is the **triceps**. This is attached to the scapula and humerus at its upper end, and to the ulna at its lower end. As this muscle lies behind the elbow joint, its contraction causes the joint to straighten, extending the arm. So the triceps is an **extensor** muscle.

Bones as levers

Figure 3.11 shows how the elbow joint, and the bones and muscles associated with it, act like a lever. The elbow joint is the pivot (fulcrum).

You may remember, from your physics studies, that forces acting across a pivot produce a *turning effect*, called a *moment*. The magnitude of the turning effect is found by multiplying the force by the distance of the point of action of the force from the pivot:

turning effect = force exerted × distance from pivot

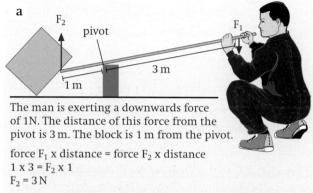

The man is exerting a downwards force of 1N. The distance of this force from the pivot is 3 m. The block is 1 m from the pivot.

force F_1 x distance = force F_2 x distance
$1 \times 3 = F_2 \times 1$
$F_2 = 3\,N$

The force on the block has therefore been multiplied by three times.

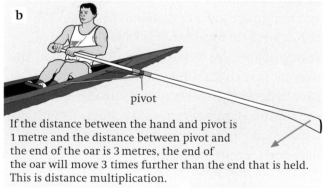

If the distance between the hand and pivot is 1 metre and the distance between pivot and the end of the oar is 3 metres, the end of the oar will move 3 times further than the end that is held. This is distance multiplication.

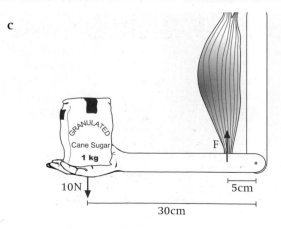

● **Figure 3.11** Turning effect and levers.
a A force multiplier. **b** A distance multiplier.
c The elbow joint – a distance multiplier.

We normally use a lever to help us to exert a large force on an object. *Figure 3.11a* shows a lever being used in this way. This kind of lever is a **force multiplier**. The relatively small force that we exert on one end of the lever is converted to a much greater force at the other end. The price we have to pay for this is that our end of the lever has to move much further than the business end – but that is not usually a problem and is well worth the extra force that we manage to produce on the object.

Figure 3.11b shows a different arrangement of a lever. Here, the end on which we exert the force is closer to the pivot. The force we need to exert on our end of the lever is actually *greater* than the force produced at the other end. However, our end of the lever does not have to move as far as the other end does. This kind of lever is called a **distance multiplier**.

Figure 3.11c is a simplified diagram of the bones and elbow joint in the human arm. Only one muscle, the biceps, is shown. When this muscle contracts, it pulls the lower arm upwards – that is, it flexes the arm. There is a heavy weight being held in the hand, so when the arm is flexed at the elbow joint this weight is lifted upwards.

SAQ 3.3

a Calculate the turning effect exerted by the mass that is being held in the hand in *figure 3.11c*.

b Calculate the force that must be exerted by the biceps muscle, in order to lift this mass.

You can see that this arrangement is a *distance multiplier*, not a *force multiplier*. Because the biceps is attached very close to the elbow joint, the turning effect that it exerts is relatively small. However, the weight in the hand is a long way from the elbow joint, so its turning effect is much greater. The force the biceps has to exert to lift the weight is much greater than the weight itself.

This may seem like a rather bad design! We could obviously reduce the force that the biceps had to exert if it was attached a long way from the elbow joint. So why have we not evolved a biceps muscle arranged like this? One major reason is that muscles simply cannot contract over large distances. (You will see why on pages 39–42.)

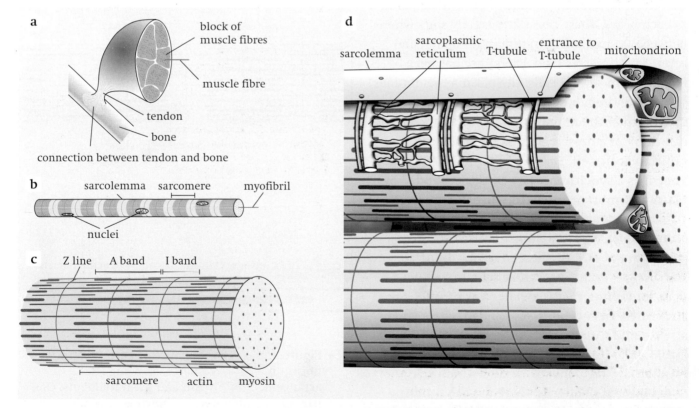

● **Figure 3.12** The structure of muscle.   **a** Part of a whole muscle.   **b** One muscle fibre. This is a syncitium, a large, multinucleate cell.   **c** A short length of one muscle fibril.   **d** A three-dimensional representation of part of a muscle fibre, showing parts of three fibrils and the sarcoplasmic reticulum.

However, they *can* produce relatively large forces. The arrangement of the biceps muscle allows a small decrease in the length of the muscle to produce a large movement in the hand (and the weight that it is carrying).

However, this is not always the best way for a joint to work. In other parts of the skeleton, muscles and bones are often arranged to work as force multipliers, not distance multipliers.

The structure and function of striated muscle

The muscle that is attached to bones, and that produces movement at joints, is known as **skeletal muscle**. When seen under the microscope it is striped, and so an alternative name for it is **striated** muscle. Cardiac muscle (the muscle in the heart) is also striated. Here, however, we will concentrate on skeletal muscle.

Muscle histology

Figure 3.12 (see page 37) shows the structure of a muscle. It is made up of many fibres, lying parallel to each other. These fibres are usually somewhere between 0.1 mm and 0.01 mm in diameter, and several centimetres long. Each fibre has been formed from several cells; the plasma membranes separating them have broken down, so that the cytoplasm of the fibre contains several nuclei. You can think of a muscle fibre as being a large, multinucleate cell. Such a structure is sometimes known as a **syncitium**. The cell is surrounded by a plasma membrane called the **sarcolemma**.

Having many nuclei is by no means the only way in which a muscle fibre differs from any other kind of cell. When seen under the microscope, each fibre can be seen to be filled with something that is arranged as parallel structures, each of which is banded with regular stripes, made up of light and dark staining bands (*figure 3.12b*). These structures are called **fibrils** (or myofibrils – 'myo' means 'to do with muscle').

In between the fibrils, there are the usual organelles you would expect to find in a cell (*figure 3.13a*). There are especially large numbers of mitochondria, as these are needed to produce the

ATP that supplies the energy for muscle contraction. Like the fibrils, these are usually arranged in a very regular fashion, lined up between adjacent fibrils. The endoplasmic reticulum, too, looks much more orderly than in a 'normal' cell. It is mostly smooth endoplasmic reticulum, and is often known as the **sarcoplasmic reticulum**. Many of the cisternae of the sarcoplasmic reticulum lie just beneath the

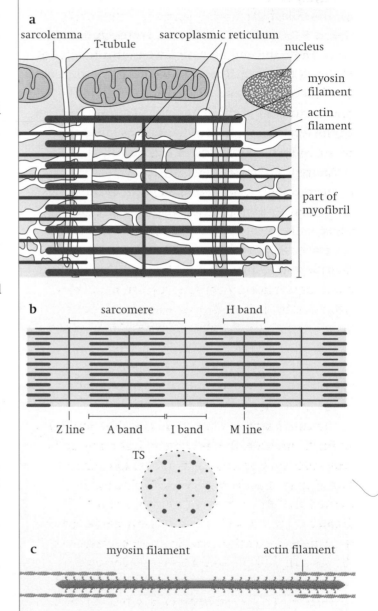

- **Figure 3.13 a** The structure of part of a muscle fibril. **b** Two sarcomeres, showing the arrangement of myosin and actin filaments. One part of the sarcomere is shown as it would appear in transverse section. **c** Diagram showing the relationship between one myosin filament and the neighbouring actin filaments in a sarcomere.

surfaces of the fibrils. The sarcolemma is deeply infolded to form channels that lie at right angles to the cisternae of the sarcoplasmic reticulum, and these channels are called **transverse tubules**, or T-tubules.

The structure of a fibril

The different parts of the stripes in a fibril each have their own letters (*figure 3.13b*). The broad, relatively dark bands are **A bands**, and the lighter areas are **I bands**. Each I band has a thin dark line, a **Z line**, in its centre. A less obvious line runs down the centre of the A band, and this line is an **M line**. The part of a fibril lying between two Z lines is known as a **sarcomere**. In any one muscle fibre (cell), all the sarcomeres of adjacent fibrils are lined up perfectly with each other, so the stripes match up all across the fibre.

This stripey appearance is caused by the very regular arrangement of two different sorts of protein in the fibrils. These proteins form **filaments**, which run lengthwise along the fibril.

One of these proteins is a fibrous protein called **myosin**, and it forms **thick filaments**. Each thick filament is made up of many myosin molecules, lying side by side. Each myosin molecule has a 'head', and the molecules are arranged in bundles so that half of the heads are at one end, and half at the other (*figure 3.13c*). The place at which the 'tails' of the myosin molecules meet each other forms the M line.

The **thin filaments** are made from the protein **actin**. Actin is a globular protein, but many actin molecules link up together to form long chains. Two chains of actin molecules lie side by side, twisted around each other, to form a thin filament. The actin chains are firmly anchored in the Z lines. Two other proteins also contribute to the structure of the thin filaments. These are **tropomyosin**, which forms a long, thin molecule that lies in the groove between the two chains of actin molecules, and **troponin**, a globular protein which binds to the actin chains at regular intervals along them (*figure 3.14b* overleaf).

You can see, in *figure 3.13b*, the extreme regularity with which the thick and thin filaments are arranged. This is what makes striated muscle look stripey. Where both actin and myosin filaments are present, the fibril looks relatively dark, producing the A bands. Where only actin is present, the fibril looks lighter, producing the I bands. You can also see that part of the A band is not quite so dark as the rest of it, and this is the region where only myosin filaments are present; it is known as the **H band**.

SAQ 3.4

Figure 3.13b shows the appearance of part of a sarcomere when seen in transverse section.
a Which band of the sarcomere is shown?
b Draw diagrams to show what the other parts of a sarcomere would look like in transverse section.

How muscle contracts

When a muscle contracts, the thin filaments in each sarcomere slide in between the thick filaments (*figure 3.14*). This shortens the sarcomere. In a relaxed muscle fibre (that is, one that is not contracting), each sarcomere is about 2.5 µm long. When the muscle contracts, the sliding of the filaments can shorten each sarcomere to about 2.0 µm.

The force which makes this happen is generated in the heads of the myosin molecules. The myosin heads act as enzymes that catalyse the hydrolysis of ATP to ADP and P_i – in other words, they are ATPases. When a fibre is relaxing, ADP and P_i are bound to each myosin head.

When a nerve impulse arrives at the muscle, a sequence of events takes place (described below) that results in the head of the myosin molecule binding to its neighbouring actin filament. The head of the myosin molecule then quickly tilts through 45°. It is still attached to the actin filament while it is doing this, so the actin filament gets pulled along towards the centre of the sarcomere. As the myosin head tilts, the ADP and P_i that were bound to it are released, and an ATP molecule takes their place. The myosin head hydrolyses this ATP to ADP and P_i, and the energy generated from this is used to detach the myosin head from the actin molecule. The head flips back to its original position, binds again to the actin molecule, pulls it along, detaches, rebinds ... over and over again. About five such cycles can happen in one second.

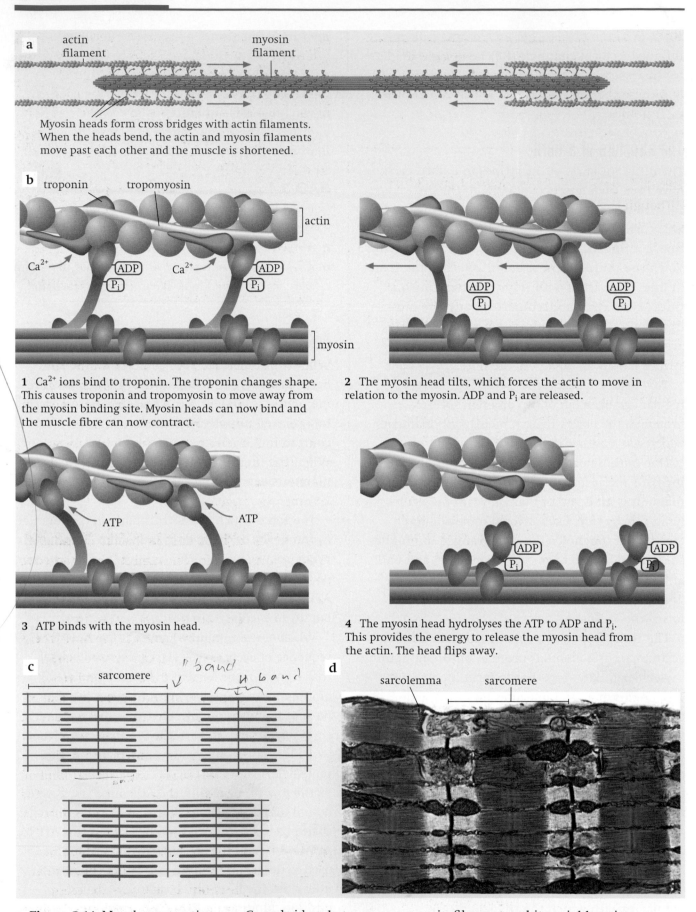

a

actin filament   myosin filament

Myosin heads form cross bridges with actin filaments. When the heads bend, the actin and myosin filaments move past each other and the muscle is shortened.

b

troponin   tropomyosin

actin

Ca^{2+} ADP Ca^{2+} ADP
            P_i P_i

myosin

ADP   ADP
P_i P_i

1 Ca^{2+} ions bind to troponin. The troponin changes shape. This causes troponin and tropomyosin to move away from the myosin binding site. Myosin heads can now bind and the muscle fibre can now contract.

2 The myosin head tilts, which forces the actin to move in relation to the myosin. ADP and P_i are released.

ATP   ATP

ADP   ADP
P_i P_i

3 ATP binds with the myosin head.

4 The myosin head hydrolyses the ATP to ADP and P_i. This provides the energy to release the myosin head from the actin. The head flips away.

c

sarcomere

d

sarcolemma   sarcomere

● **Figure 3.14** Muscle contraction.   **a** Cross bridges between one myosin filament and its neighbouring actin filaments.   **b** How myosin causes the actin filaments to slide.   **c** The appearance of a sarcomere in relaxed (top) and contracted muscle.   **d** Electronmicrograph of contracted muscle ($\times 20\,000$).

SAQ 3.5

After death, the supply of ATP in a muscle cell gradually runs out. With reference to the interaction of myosin and actin, suggest how this can explain the development of rigor mortis (muscular stiffening) in the few hours after death.

The force generated during muscle contraction

Although the force generated by one myosin molecule acting on one actin filament is not very big, if there are millions of myosin molecules binding to and pulling on millions of actin molecules, then you can imagine that the overall force they produce can be large. In human muscle, the maximum force that can be generated by a contracting muscle is about 40–50 N per cm² of cross-sectional area.

It would seem likely that the more myosin–actin interactions that were taking place, the larger the force they could generate. And this does seem to be the case. *Figure 3.15* shows that, during the contraction of a sarcomere, the greatest force is produced when there is the greatest overlap between the actin and myosin filaments. If a sarcomere is pulled out to such a length that there is no overlap between actin and myosin filaments, then it cannot contract at all. However, if there is at least some overlap, then a few myosin heads can interact with actin

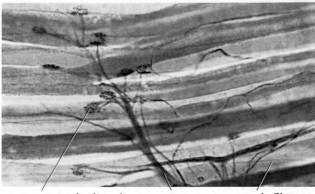

neuro-muscular junction   axon   muscle fibre

● **Figure 3.16** Light micrograph of a motor end-plate (× 200). The axon of the motor neurone is divided into several branches, which form neuromuscular junctions (nerve–muscle synapses).

filaments, and produce a small force that can begin to pull the actin filaments inwards. The overlap between the actin and myosin gets more and more, allowing more and more myosin–actin bridges to form, and so more force can be generated. But once the sarcomere has got so short that the ends of the myosin filaments have hit the Z lines, then it is impossible for any more contraction to take place.

How a nerve impulse causes muscle contraction

Skeletal muscle contracts when it is stimulated to do so by the arrival of action potentials along the axons of motor neurones. The end of the motor neurone does not make direct contact with the muscle fibre; there is a very small gap between the membrane of the axon and the plasma membrane (sarcolemma) of the muscle fibre. The area where the two membranes lie close together is called a **neuromuscular junction**, and it is really just a special kind of synapse (*Biology 1*, pages 116–17). The motor neurone axon divides into several branches, forming a **motor end-plate** (*figure 3.16*). One neurone may form neuromuscular junctions with several different muscle fibres, but each muscle fibre is only innervated by a single motor neurone.

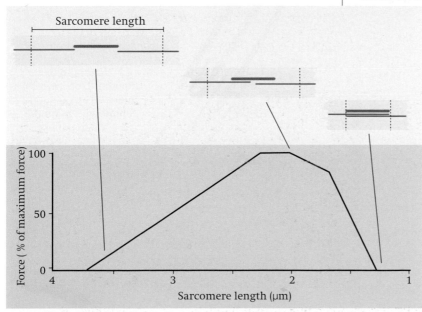

● **Figure 3.15** Forces generated during different stages of sarcomere contraction.

When an action potential arrives at the presynaptic membrane at a neuromuscular junction (that is the membrane at the end of the motor neurone's axon), it causes calcium ions to flood into the axon. These calcium ions cause vesicles of neurotransmitter substance – normally acetylcholine – to empty their contents into the synaptic cleft. The acetylcholine diffuses across the cleft, and binds with receptor proteins in the sarcolemma. This causes sodium channels to open, so that sodium ions flood in and depolarise the sarcolemma. This is all just the same as the events that occur at any cholinergic synapse.

The depolarisation spreads rapidly across the whole of the sarcolemma. You may remember that there are infoldings of the sarcolemma that reach deep into the fibre, called T-tubules. The depolarisation spreads along these, so that it is carried right into the centre of the muscle fibre. Here it is transmitted to the membranes of the sarcoplasmic reticulum (*figure 3.17*).

When a muscle is resting, transporter proteins in the membranes of the sarcoplasmic reticulum move calcium ions into the cisternae, by active transport. When an action potential arrives, it causes these membranes to become permeable to calcium ions. They flood out of the cisternae down their concentration gradient, and diffuse in amongst the fibrils.

The calcium ions bind with the troponin molecules on the thin (actin) filaments. This makes the troponin molecules change shape. As they do so, they make the tropomyosin molecules move, exposing a site on the actin filament to which myosin heads can bind. This then sets off the binding–tilting–releasing cycle described earlier.

When action potentials stop arriving at the muscle fibre, the sarcolemma and T-tubules are no longer depolarised, and the calcium channels of the sarcoplasmic reticulum close. Calcium ions can no longer move out of the cisternae, and, indeed, the transporter proteins in the membranes of the sarcoplasmic reticulum rapidly begin to push them back in again. So the calcium ions bound to the troponin are released, the tropomyosin moves back into its normal position, covering the myosin binding sites on the actin filaments, and the myosin heads can no longer bind. The muscle is relaxed.

Once a sarcomere has contracted, it will stay in this position – even after action potentials stop

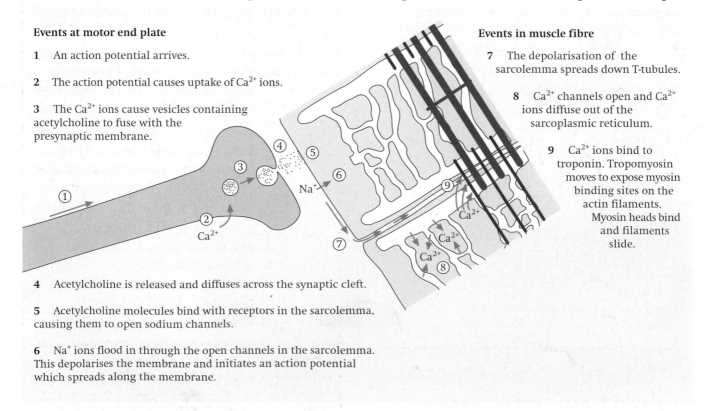

Events at motor end plate

1   An action potential arrives.

2   The action potential causes uptake of Ca^{2+} ions.

3   The Ca^{2+} ions cause vesicles containing acetylcholine to fuse with the presynaptic membrane.

4   Acetylcholine is released and diffuses across the synaptic cleft.

5   Acetylcholine molecules bind with receptors in the sarcolemma, causing them to open sodium channels.

6 Na^+ ions flood in through the open channels in the sarcolemma. This depolarises the membrane and initiates an action potential which spreads along the membrane.

Events in muscle fibre

7   The depolarisation of the sarcolemma spreads down T-tubules.

8 Ca^{2+} channels open and Ca^{2+} ions diffuse out of the sarcoplasmic reticulum.

9 Ca^{2+} ions bind to troponin. Tropomyosin moves to expose myosin binding sites on the actin filaments. Myosin heads bind and filaments slide.

● **Figure 3.17** How a nerve impulse causes muscle contraction.

arriving – unless something pulls it back again. The 'something' may be an antagonistic muscle, or it may be a weight or other force acting on it.

Energy for muscle contraction

We have seen that ATP provides the energy that allows the repetitive binding, tilting and releasing of the myosin heads, and thus the force that causes muscle contraction. ATP is the only substance that can do this – nothing else will do.

ATP is produced by respiration. A muscle normally contains only a relatively small amount of ATP. If you run in a sprint race, you will use up all of the ATP in your leg muscles in the first three or four seconds (*figure 3.18*). Your muscles then need to produce more ATP if you are to continue running. They first do this using their small store of **creatine phosphate**, which can lose its phosphate group and transfer it to ADP to produce more ATP. This creatine phosphate may be enough to see you through the rest of the race. So far, you may notice, your muscles have not needed to respire at all – they are using ATP and creatine phosphate that were already there. Top-class sprinters often run the whole of a 100 m race without breathing.

However, if you still need to keep moving, another way of producing ATP must be found. If there is sufficient oxygen being delivered to the muscles, they can break down glucose in aerobic respiration. Muscles contain glycogen stores

which can be as much as 2 % of the muscle mass, and which can provide enough glucose to make all the ATP you need to last for several hours of activity. Once this store is used up, glycogen stores in the liver can be broken down to produce more glucose that can be transported to the muscles. Muscles are also able to respire fatty acids.

If insufficient oxygen is available, then glucose is broken down anaerobically. This can not go on for long, however, because it produces lactic acid, which is toxic if it builds up in high concentrations. The lactic acid is transported to the liver, which breaks it down when oxygen becomes available (see *Biology 2*, pages 12–13).

> **Box 3A Twitch and tonic muscle fibres**
> All vertebrates, including humans and other mammals, have two different types of muscle fibres, known as twitch (or fast twitch) fibres and tonic (or slow twitch) fibres. Most muscles contain a mixture of the two types of fibre.
>
> Twitch fibres are used for fast contraction. They are adapted for movements requiring quick, strong contraction that lasts only for a short time, such as in jumping. They can work for a few seconds up to a minute or so, and are therefore important in any rapid, powerful movement such as sprinting.
>
> Tonic fibres are used for slow, prolonged contraction. They are used for maintaining posture, and also for movements which take place over a relatively long period of time, such as distance running.
>
> Twitch fibres hydrolyse ATP very rapidly, and they produce most of their ATP by glycolysis. They contain relatively few mitochondria, and relatively small amounts of myoglobin. They therefore appear white rather than red (myoglobin, like haemoglobin, is a red pigment). They have more extensive sarcoplasmic reticulum than tonic fibres, and are able to actively transport calcium ions faster than tonic fibres can. They have relatively large diameters, about twice the diameter of a tonic fibre.
>
> Tonic fibres hydrolyse ATP relatively slowly, and they produce most of their ATP by aerobic respiration. They contain large numbers of mitochondria, and large amounts of myoglobin, which makes them appear red. Their relatively small diameter provides a short distance over which oxygen has to diffuse from the blood into the mitochondria. The number of capillaries close to a group of tonic fibres is much greater than that associated with twitch fibres, which again makes muscle containing tonic fibres look redder than muscle containing twitch fibres.

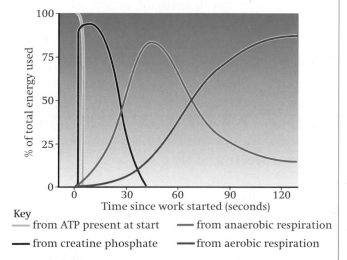

Key
—— from ATP present at start
—— from creatine phosphate
—— from anaerobic respiration
—— from aerobic respiration

● **Figure 3.18** Energy sources used in a muscle during exercise.

Effects of ageing on the locomotory system

Many changes occur in our bodies as we age. A number of these changes involve bones, joints and muscles, and we will here look at two results of these changes – osteoarthritis and osteoporosis.

Osteoarthritis

Arthritis is a general term for a disease that affects the joints ('artho' means 'to do with joints') and causes pain and loss of movement in them.

There are several different types of arthritis. One of these is rheumatoid arthritis, in which the body's own immune system treats the cartilage at joint surfaces as if it were an invading organism; it is an autoimmune disease. Rheumatoid arthritis is most common in people with a gene called HLA-DR4, and it is probable that other genes are also linked with a person's likelihood of suffering from this disease.

Osteoarthritis, on the other hand, does not appear to have any genetic link, nor is it an autoimmune disease. In a person with osteoarthritis, the normally very smooth surface of the cartilage at joints becomes rougher, making joint movement less easy and sometimes very painful (*figure 3.19*). Some degeneration of the cartilage at joints happens in everyone as they age, so that almost anyone over the age of 60 has some degree of roughening of the cartilage in their joints. In most people, though, this is not enough to produce any more than very mild symptoms. The term 'osteoarthritis' is normally only used when the degeneration gets so bad that there is significant pain and loss of mobility.

In osteoarthritis, changes occur in the collagen and glycoproteins that help to give cartilage its resilience, so that these gradually break down. At the same time, the normal balance between the gradual breakdown and replacement of cartilage is disrupted, so that breakdown happens faster than replacement. The result is a loss of cartilage from the surface of bones at joints, and also a reduction in the flexibility and resilience of the cartilage that remains. It becomes increasingly painful to move the joint, and eventually movement at some joints may be completely lost.

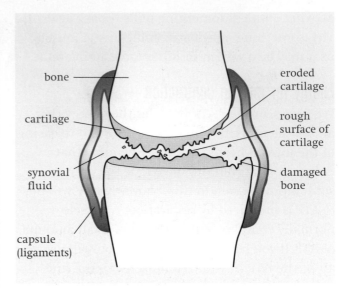

● **Figure 3.19** A joint affected by osteoarthritis.

The joints that are most frequently affected are those in the hands, knees and hips.

Despite much research, it is still not at all clear why some people develop osteoarthritis while others do not. There is some evidence that the way joints are used early in life may affect this. For example, people who play sports or dance professionally, where there is repeated and vigorous bending of the knees, seem to be more likely to suffer from osteoarthritis in the knee joints later in life. This is also true if the joints suffered an injury, particularly twisting injuries in the knee. Overweight people are also more likely to develop osteoarthritis, especially in the load-bearing joints at knees and hips.

The pain and inflammation at arthritic joints can be partly relieved by non-steroidal anti-inflammatory drugs, such as aspirin. These reduce pain, stiffness and swelling. However, for long-term relief the only option is joint replacement. Such surgery is now very successful, and people with joint replacements can often return to the degree of mobility that they had before osteoarthritis set in.

Osteoporosis

Like osteoarthritis, osteoporosis is a degenerative disease that results from an inbalance in the normal breakdown and rebuilding of skeletal tissues. Here, however, the tissue that is affected is bone, rather than cartilage.

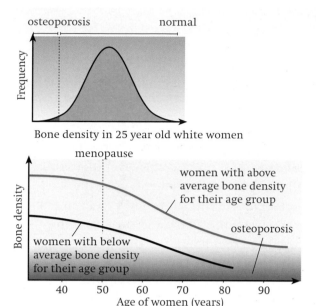

● **Figure 3.20** Variation of bone density with age.

Some loss of bone mass with age is absolutely normal. Maximum bone mass occurs around the age of 30 for most people, after which it slowly decreases (*figure 3.20*). The average rate of loss is probably about 7% per year in an adult, and tends to be more rapid in women who are past the menopause than in men or in pre-menopausal women. Bone density gradually decreases, as the rate of activity of the osteoblasts that build bone becomes less than that of the osteoclasts that break it down. For most people, however, this natural loss of bone mass does not cause significant problems. The term 'osteoporosis' is reserved for a condition in which so much bone mass is lost that the bones become much more likely to break. One definition of osteoporosis is a condition in which bone density is less than 648 mg cm^{-3}. Normal bone density is at least 833 mg cm^{-3}.

Osteoporosis is a widespread and common disease. In the United States of America, one in two women and one in five men over the age of 65 will suffer a broken bone due to osteoporosis. Usually a person has no idea that they have osteoporosis until a bone breaks. For example, a sudden strain may cause a limb bone to fracture or a vertebra to collapse. A fall that would be nothing to a younger person may cause a hip bone to break in an older person with osteoporosis.

There is evidence that having a high bone density and bone mass when you are younger can reduce the risk of suffering from osteoporosis when you are older. To achieve a high bone density, people need to exercise regularly, as bone growth responds to the forces that regularly act on the bones. Diet is also important; diets lacking in calcium or vitamin D can result in poor mineralisation of bone. The best source of calcium is dairy products such as milk and cheese, but unfortunately many young people avoid these foods because they see them as 'fattening', or likely to increase their cholesterol levels. Women who diet and keep their weight artificially low when they are young may be more likely to suffer from osteoporosis in their old age. Cigarette smoking also appears to increase the risk of osteoporosis (*figure 3.21*).

Women are more likely to develop osteoporosis than men. This may be partly because their bone mass is less throughout their lives, so they can afford to lose less bone as they age. Loss of bone mass in women speeds up after they have reached menopause, when their ovaries no longer secrete oestrogen. Hormone replacement therapy, in which oestrogen and progesterone are taken regularly after the menopause, can considerably reduce the risk of osteoporosis.

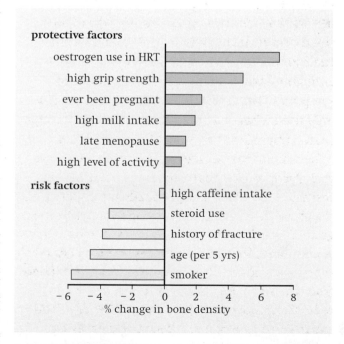

● **Figure 3.21** Risk factors and protective factors for osteoporosis.

SUMMARY

◆ The human skeleton is an endoskeleton, made from bone and cartilage.

◆ Compact bone is formed by cells called osteoblasts, which secrete tropocollagen which naturally polymerises to form collagen. Calcium phosphate also builds up around these cells, which are now known as osteocytes. The cells and their surrounding matrix are arranged in circular groups known as Haversian systems. The composite nature of the matrix of bone gives it flexibility, and strength in tension and in compression.

◆ Hyaline cartilage is laid down by cells known as chondrocytes, which secrete tropocollagen and glycoproteins. These give cartilage strength and flexibility.

◆ The vertebral column is made up of 33 vertebrae, separated from each other by cartilage discs. A lumbar vertebra has a thick centrum and short, strong transverse processes and neural spine. A thoracic vertebra has a lighter construction, with a long backwardly-pointing neural spine. The spinal cord runs through the neural arches of the vertebrae. Vertebrae are held together by ligaments, and articulate with each other via processes on their surfaces. A thoracic vertebra has extra processes for articulation with the ribs.

◆ The five-fingered or pentadactyl limb that is found in all amphibians, reptiles, birds and mammals is strong evidence that they share a common ancestry.

◆ A joint occurs wherever two bones meet. Joints may be immoveable (as in the skull), allow restricted movement (as in the vertebral column), allow movement in one plane (as at the elbow and knee) or allow circular movement (as at the shoulder and hip). Joints where significant movement occurs are known as synovial joints.

◆ The elbow joint is a hinge synovial joint. The bones are held together by ligaments, and the joint is enclosed in a capsule whose inner surface is lined by a synovial membrane, which secretes synovial fluid. Friction is further reduced by a layer of exceptionally smooth hyaline cartilage on the ends of the bones.

◆ Movement across the elbow joint is produced by the contraction of flexor muscles (the biceps and brachialis) and extensor muscles (such as the triceps). These are antagonistic muscles. Muscles are joined to bones by tendons. The bones, muscles and joint of the arm act as a distance multiplier.

- Skeletal (striated) muscle is made up of long multinucleated cells called fibres. The plasma membrane of a muscle fibre is known as the sarcolemma, and has deep inward folds called T-tubules. Inside each fibre there are many fibrils, containing thick filaments of myosin and thin filaments of actin, troponin and tropomyosin. These are arranged to form a repeating pattern of bands. The distance from one Z line to another forms one sarcomere.

- Muscles contract as the myosin filaments attach to actin filaments and pull them in towards the centre of the sarcomere. The energy for this comes from ATP, which is hydrolysed by the heads of the myosin molecules.

- Contraction in skeletal muscle is initiated by the arrival of an action potential, which crosses a neuromuscular junction and depolarises the sarcolemma. This causes calcium ions to be released into the fibrils, which interact with troponin in such a way as to allow myosin to bind with actin.

- Osteoarthritis and osteoporosis are degenerative diseases whose incidence is more common in elderly people. In osteoarthritis, the cartilage at joints is damaged and not replaced, resulting in pain and loss of mobility. In osteoporosis, the density of bone decreases, increasing the likelihood of bone fractures.

Questions

1 Outline the roles of each of the following proteins in the structure and function of the human locomotory system:
   a collagen;
   b actin and myosin;
   c troponin and tropomyosin.

2 Explain the meaning of each of the following terms:
   a Haversian system;
   b chondrocyte;
   c pentadactyl limb;
   d sarcoplasmic reticulum;
   e osteoporosis.

3 Compare the structure of compact bone and hyaline cartilage, and explain how the differences between them relate to their functions.

4 a With reference to the elbow joint, explain how the structure and arrangement of the bones and muscles in the arm allow flexion and extension of the arm to be brought about.
   b Describe the changes that take place in a joint in the disease osteoarthritis, and explain the effects of these changes.

5 a With the aid of diagrams, describe the structure of skeletal (striated) muscle.
   b Explain how the arrival of an action potential at a neuromuscular junction may result in muscle contraction.

CHAPTER 4

The nervous system

By the end of this chapter you should be able to:

1 describe the organisation of the nervous system with reference to the central and the peripheral systems;

2 outline the organisation of the autonomic nervous system into a sympathetic and a parasympathetic system;

3 outline the roles of the autonomic nervous system in controlling the digestive system, heart action and the size of the pupil in the eye;

4 describe the gross structure of the human brain;

5 outline the functions of the cerebrum, hypothalamus, cerebellum and medulla oblongata;

6 describe the symptoms and possible causes of Alzheimer's disease as an example of brain malfunction.

In some animals, such as cnidarians (jellyfish, sea anemones and their relatives) the nervous system is made up of a simple network of neurones. However, in all vertebrates, as well as in many non-vertebrate animals, the nervous system has a much more sophisticated organisation, in which some parts are specialised for processing and integrating information, while other parts are specialised for transmitting information rapidly from receptors and to effectors. In this chapter, we will look at the structural and functional organisation of the human nervous system, and also consider one example of a common illness which results when one small part of it malfunctions.

The organisation of the human nervous system

The mammalian nervous system is made up of two major types of cells – **neurones** and **glial cells**. The neurones are specialised for transmitting information, in the form of **action potentials**

(sometimes called nerve impulses). The glial cells have a variety of functions such as helping nutrients to pass from the blood to the neurones, helping to maintain the correct balance of ions in the tissue fluid that surrounds them, and perhaps also destroying potential pathogens by phagocytosis. The Schwann cells that form the myelination around some dendrons and axons (*Biology 2*, pages 106–7) are glial cells. Recent research suggests that glial cells may also play a role in stimulating the formation of synapses, an important feature of memory (page 89).

In chapter 6 in *Biology 2*, we looked at the detailed structure of a neurone, how action potentials pass along neurones – including the roles of synapses – and how information is passed from a receptor to an effector in a reflex arc. In this chapter, rather than considering the detail of how individual neurones function, we are going to look at the way in which the whole nervous system is organised, in terms of both structure and function, in a human.

The human nervous sytem is made up of two main components. The **central nervous system**

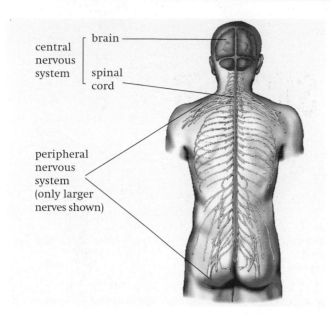

● **Figure 4.1** The human nervous system.

(often abbreviated to CNS) comprises the brain and spinal cord, while the **peripheral nervous system** includes all the neurones that lie outside these organs (*figure 4.1*).

The central nervous system

Within the central nervous system, most neurones are intermediate neurones, with many short dendrites (*figure 4.2*). They have many synapses with other neighbouring neurones – sometimes as many as 200 000. The function of these neurones is to receive and integrate information arriving via these synapses, and then to pass on action potentials to other neurones. Some of the synapses are excitatory – in other words, when an action potential arrives at them, this depolarises the postsynaptic membrane. Some are inhibitory – the arrival of an action potential *prevents* the postsynaptic membrane from depolarising. Within the neurone, therefore, the balance between excitation and inhibition that is happening at all the synapses will determine whether or not the neurone passes an action potential along its axon to other neurones. As there are around 200×10^{12} neurones in a human brain, you can probably imagine that the possible number of different patterns of excitation and inhibition of different neurones is, to all intents and purposes, infinite.

The **spinal cord** extends from the base of the brain, down through the neural arches of the vertebrae, as far as the first lumbar vertebra. In the centre of it is a canal containing **cerebrospinal fluid**. A butterfly-shaped region in the centre of the cord contains unmyelinated neurones, and thus appears grey. Around this the axons and dendrons of the neurones are mostly myelinated, and this area appears white.

The **brain** can be considered to be a highly specialised extension of the spinal cord. Its structure is described in detail on pages 54–7.

Both brain and spinal cord are surrounded by three membranes known as **meninges**. These membranes help to secrete the cerebrospinal fluid, which fills all the spaces inside the brain and spinal cord, and also the space beneath the skull bones. The fluid helps to absorb mechanical shocks to the brain (such as when you hit your head on something) and also to provide nutrients and oxygen to the brain cells.

The peripheral nervous system

The peripheral nervous system is made up of sensory neurones that carry action potentials from receptors towards the central nervous system, and motor neurones that carry action potentials from the central nervous system to effectors.

The cell bodies of sensory neurones are situated just outside the spinal cord, in the dorsal root ganglia. (A ganglion is a

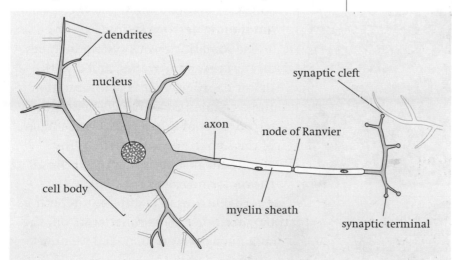

● **Figure 4.2** A neurone in the central nervous system.

group of nerve cell bodies.) They have long cytoplasmic processes that pick up information at receptors (for example sense organs in the skin) and transmit action potentials from the receptor towards their cell bodies. From here, action potentials pass along their axons into the central nervous system. The cell bodies of many motor neurones are in the spinal cord and their long axons pass out of the spinal cord and towards effectors such as muscles or glands.

In the peripheral nervous system, axons and dendrons are arranged in bundles called **nerves**. Any one nerve can contain a variety of dendrons carrying information from receptors, and axons carrying information to effectors. *Figure 4.3* is a micrograph of a transverse section through a nerve.

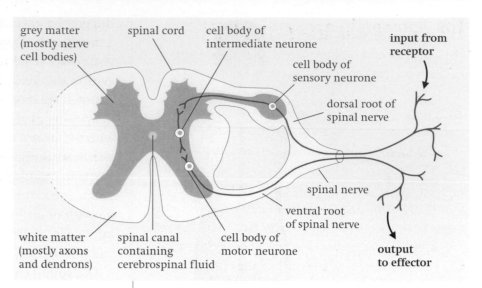

● **Figure 4.4** Diagrammatic section of the spinal cord and a spinal nerve, showing the arrangements of neurones forming a reflex arc.

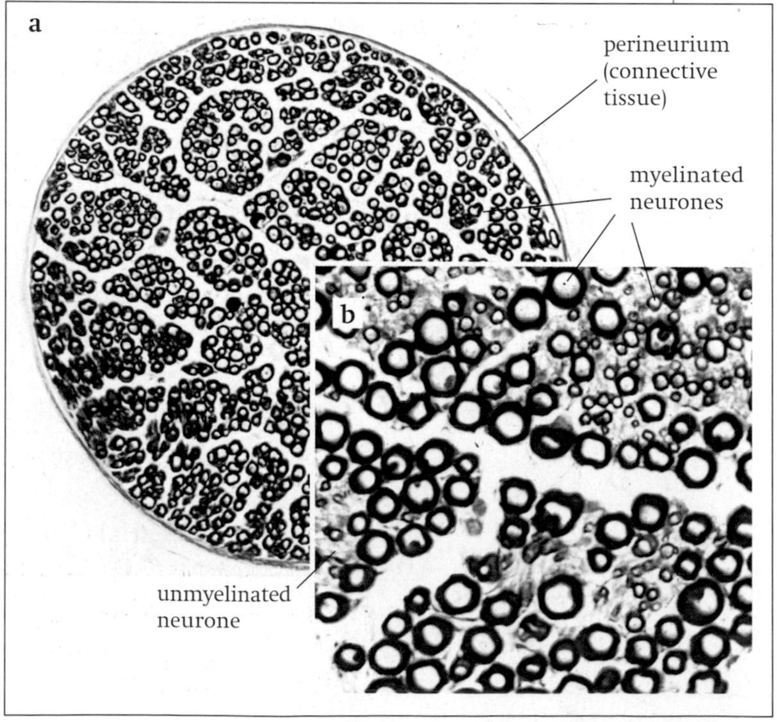

SAQ 4.1

Explain the difference between a *neurone* and a *nerve*.

Axons and dendrons leave and enter the spinal cord in **spinal nerves**, which occur in between each pair of vertebrae. Each spinal nerve has a **dorsal root**, which carries impulses from receptors towards the spinal cord, and a **ventral root**, which carries impulses outwards to effectors. Nerves that arise from the brain are known as **cranial nerves**.

The peripheral nervous system is made up of two different systems. These are the **somatic nervous system** and the **autonomic nervous system**.

The somatic nervous system includes all the sensory neurones, and also the motor neurones that take information to the skeletal muscles. So the neurones in a typical reflex arc (*figure 4.4*) are all part of the somatic nervous system. The autonomic nervous system includes all the motor neurones that supply the internal organs. It is different in both its organisation and its functions from the somatic nervous system, and we now look at this in detail.

● **Figure 4.3 a** Transverse section through a nerve (× 100), containing hundreds of axons and dendrons.
b Enlargement of part of the nerve shown in **a** (× 300). The axons and dendrons with the darkly-stained, thickened edges are myelinated, and the others are unmyelinated.

The autonomic nervous system

The autonomic nervous system includes all the motor neurones that take information to the viscera – that is the internal organs. It controls the activity of all the smooth muscle in the body, for example in the walls of arterioles and in the wall of the alimentary canal. It also controls the rate of beating of the cardiac muscle in the heart, and the activities of exocrine glands such as the salivary glands. 'Autonomic' means 'self-adjusting', and this refers to the fact that most of the activities that are controlled by the autonomic nervous system are not usually under our voluntary control.

As well as having a different *function* from the somatic nervous system, the autonomic nervous system also has a different *structural organisation* (*figure 4.5*). As we have already seen, the motor neurones of the somatic nervous system have their cell bodies in the central nervous system, and long axons that lead from these cell bodies all the way to an effector. The cell bodies of the motor neurones of the autonomic nervous

system, however, have their cell bodies outside the central nervous system, in **autonomic ganglia**. Another type of neurone, called a **preganglionic** neurone, carries action potentials from the central nervous system to this ganglion.

The autonomic nervous system is itself divided into two components – the sympathetic and parasympathetic systems – and we will look at these in turn (*figure 4.6*).

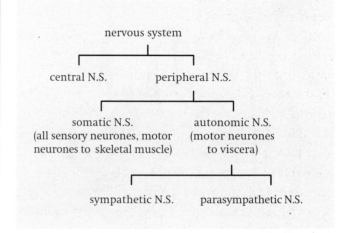

● **Figure 4.6** The components of the human nervous system.

a

Somatic motor pathway

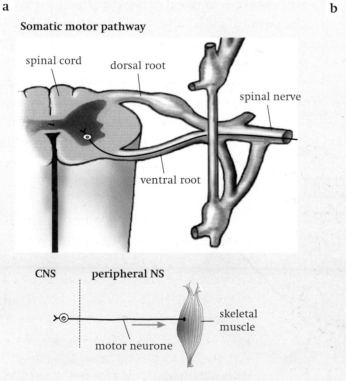

b

Autonomic pathway – (sympathetic)

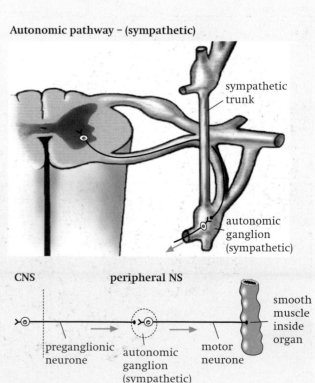

● **Figure 4.5** The layout of motor pathways (that is, the pathways along which impulses travel from the CNS to an effector) in **a** the somatic system and **b** the autonomic system. In each case, the actual arrangement of the spinal cord and nerves is shown at the top, and a diagrammatic simplification appears below.

The sympathetic nervous system

Figure 4.7 shows the structure of the **sympathetic nervous system**. We have already seen that the cell bodies of its motor neurones lie in ganglia outside the spinal cord. The axons of the pre-ganglionic neurones pass out of the spinal cord through the ventral root, and synapse with the motor neurone cell bodies in these ganglia. There are also neurones that directly connect each ganglion with the next.

From these ganglia, axons pass to all the organs within the body. Here they form synapses with the muscles (cardiac muscle in the heart, smooth muscle elsewhere). The transmitter substance that carries the impulse across most of these synapses is **noradrenaline** (which is almost the same as adrenaline, and is also known as **epinephrine**). You will probably not be surprised, therefore, that the effects of nerve impulses arriving at organs via the sympathetic nervous system are often to *stimulate* them. For example, they cause the heart to beat faster, the pupils to dilate and the bronchi to dilate. All of these responses are very similar to those which result from secretion of the hormone adrenaline, and which can be summarised as 'fight or flight' responses. However, not all effects of the sympathetic nervous system are stimulatory, as you can see in *Table 4.1*.

Some neurones in the sympathetic system use **acetylcholine** as the neurotransmitter that carries impulses to effector organs. These include the sweat glands, the erector muscles in the skin, and some blood vessels. The effects are still mostly stimulatory, causing the sweat glands to produce more sweat and the erector muscles to make the hairs stand on end.

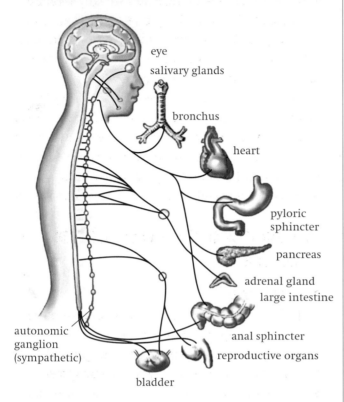

- **Figure 4.7** The stucture of the sympathetic nervous system.

Organ		Effect of sympathetic stimulation	Effect of parasympathetic stimulation
heart		increases rate and force of contraction	reduces rate and force of contraction
eye	pupil	dilates (gets wider)	constricts (gets narrower)
	ciliary muscles	relax, which makes the lens thinner for distant vision	contract, which makes the lens thicker for near vision
digestive system	glands	little or no effect	stimulates secretion
	sphincter muscles	contraction	relaxation
	liver	release of glucose to blood	small increase in glycogen production
skin	sweat glands	increases sweating	little effect, except to increase sweating on palms of hands
	erector muscles	contract, making hairs stand on end	no effect
	arterioles	vasoconstriction	no effect

- **Table 4.1** Some effects of the sympathetic and parasympathetic nervous systems.

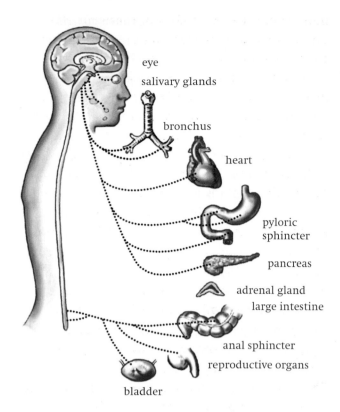

eye
salivary glands
bronchus
heart
pyloric sphincter
pancreas
adrenal gland
large intestine
anal sphincter
reproductive organs
bladder

● **Figure 4.8** The structure of the parasympathetic nervous system.

SAQ 4.2

Explain how the effects of the sympathetic nervous system help to prepare the body for fast action in a dangerous situation.

The parasympathetic nervous system

Figure 4.8 shows the structure of the **parasympathetic nervous system**. Unlike the sympathetic system, the nerve pathways involved in the parasympathetic system all begin in the brain, the top of the spinal cord, or the very base of the spinal cord.

As in the sympathetic system, two different neurones carry the impulse on its way from the central nervous system to the effector organ. However, whereas the synapses between these neurones in the sympathetic system are inside ganglia close to the spinal cord, this is not so in the parasympathetic system. Instead, the neurone that carries the impulse out of the brain or spinal cord just keeps on going, until it is right inside the wall of the organ that it will stimulate. It is

here, actually in the organ, that this neurone synapses with the effector neurone.

Many of the axons of the neurones of the parasympathetic nervous system are in the **vagus nerves**, which leave the brain and carry information to all of the organs in the thorax and abdomen.

The neurotransmitter released into the organs from the parasympathetic axons is **acetylcholine**. This often has an inhibitory effect on the activities of the organ. Once again, however, the situation is not entirely cut-and-dried, and you will see from *table 4.1* that impulses arriving through the parasympathetic system have an inhibitory effect on some organs, and a stimulatory effect on others.

It may help to remember that the sympathetic nervous system tends to prepare the body for 'fight or flight', while the parasympathetic nervous system tends to help it to 'rest and digest'.

Some examples of effects of the autonomic nervous system

The digestive system

The walls of the alimentary canal contain nerve endings from both the sympathetic and parasympathetic nervous systems. In general, stimulation from the parasympathetic system tends to stimulate activity, by causing sphincter muscles to open and causing the smooth muscle involved in peristalsis to contract. It also causes the salivary glands and gastric glands to increase their secretion of saliva and gastric juice.

SAQ 4.3

Suggest one stimulus which might result in action potentials being carried to the salivary glands via the parasympathetic nervous system.

The sympathetic nervous system is not normally very significant in the working of the alimentary canal. Strong stimulation from it can, however, reduce peristalsis and cause sphincters to close, so that food passes through the digestive system much more slowly. It can also have an indirect effect on the secretory glands, because it can bring about vasoconstriction (narrowing) of the blood vessels that supply them, thus reducing their rate of secretion.

The action of the heart

You will remember that cardiac muscle is myogenic – that is, it contracts and relaxes automatically with no need for stimulation by the nervous system. The patch of muscle known as the **sino-atrial node** (SAN), in the wall of the right atrium, has a faster natural rate of contraction than all the other muscle in the heart, so the SAN sets the rhythm for the rest of the heart muscle.

The SAN receives impulses from both the sympathetic and parasympathetic nervous systems. Impulses from the latter reach it via the vagus nerve. Impulses arriving from the sympathetic system increase the rate of contraction of the SAN, and therefore the whole heart. This also increases the force of contraction of the heart muscle, so the overall effect is for the heart to beat faster and to push more blood into the arteries with each beat. Impulses from the parasympathetic system have exactly the opposite effects.

SAQ 4.4

Suggest how parasympathetic stimulation of the SAN might affect blood pressure.

The pupil in the eye

The pupil is the dark space in the centre of the iris (*figure 4.9*). The iris contains circular and radial muscles, and their activity can widen or narrow the diameter of the pupil. It tends to widen in dim light, to allow more light onto the retina, and to narrow in bright light, to prevent too much light damaging the cells within the retina.

Stimulation from the sympathetic system causes the radial muscle fibres in the iris to contract, thus widening the pupil. This can happen if a person is excited or nervous, as well as when light is dim. Stimulation from the parasympathetic system causes the circular muscles to contract, thus narrowing the pupil. This can be a reflex action resulting from stimulation of the retina with very bright light.

The brain

The human brain is currently, as it always has been, an object of tremendous interest. Events occurring in the human brain underlie all of our behaviour. We would love to know how these events affect what we do. How do we perceive, think, learn and remember? What exactly is 'consciousness'? How does the brain control behaviour such as walking and talking, and our emotions such as anger, fear, love, happiness and despair?

Considerable progress has been made in recent years in our knowledge of the anatomy and physiology of the brain, and we are beginning to understand a little about how they may affect behaviour. However, we are still a very long way from being able to explain precisely how even such simple behaviour as walking is controlled, let alone more complex behaviour such as the creation of works of art.

How the brain is studied

The anatomy and histology of the human brain is relatively easy to study. Many people allow their organs, including the brain, to be used for research after their death, and from such research we now know a great deal about the overall structure of the brain, and also its detailed structure in terms of the types of cells found in different parts of it. However, the enormous numbers of cells, and the huge numbers of connections between them, mean that it is not possible to trace every single pathway along which impulses could travel in the brain. The best that we can do is to identify particular *groups* of neurones in different parts of the brain, and attempt to trace how such groups are connected to other groups.

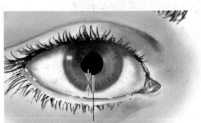

radial muscle contracts with sympathetic stimulation

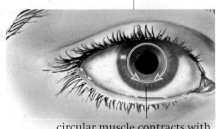

circular muscle contracts with parasympathetic stimulation

● **Figure 4.9** The effects of sympathetic and parasympathetic stimulation on the iris.

In the past, the only way in which anything could be learned about the functions of different parts of the brain was to study the behaviour of people with brain damage. For example, in 1861 a French scientist, Pierre Broca, studied a person who could not speak or write intelligibly, although he could understand language that he read or heard. After this person died, Broca investigated his brain, and found that a small area near the front of the left side, now known as Broca's area, was damaged. Broca found eight other people with similar problems, and in every case discovered that the person's brain was damaged in just this place. He therefore concluded, quite correctly, that this part of the brain is responsible for the production of language. Studies of people with damaged brains – for example after a stroke, or the removal of a tumour by surgery – are still providing us with information about the localisation of brain functions. They have shown us that, while some functions seem to be carried out by particular small regions of the brain, others do not appear to have a precise location.

Studies of the brains of people with particular illnesses, both before and after their death, also help us to understand more about how the brain works. For example, we know that the brains of people with Alzheimer's disease (described on pages 61–3) contain certain groups of cells that do not secrete enough of the neurotransmitter acetylcholine, so this tells us a little about how this part of the brain, and this neurotransmitter, affect behaviour. The effects of particular chemicals (drugs) on the brain can provide leads to the structure and functions of the molecules that are involved in normal brain activity. We also have more sophisticated methods of studying the activity of the brain, including **brain scans** which

Box 4A Brain scans

Computer assisted tomography or **CAT** scans use X-rays that can distinguish between subtly different tissues, and can produce images of the distribution of these tissues in a particular 'section' through the brain. If many such sections are recorded, then computer analysis can build up a three-dimensional picture of how these tissues are distributed within the brain.

Positron emission tomography, usually known as **PET**, is a technique which can allow the activity of a living brain to be studied. A substance whose molecules are very like glucose, called 2-deoxyglucose, is introduced into the blood supply to the brain. The molecules are 'labelled' by binding with an isotope that emits positrons. Respiring brain cells take up the labelled 2-deoxyglucose, and treat it just as though it was ordinary glucose to be used in glycolysis – they phosphorylate it. However, this phosphorylated 2-deoxyglucose cannot then be metabolised any further, nor can it be removed from the cell. Scans are then made in a similar way to a CAT scan, but this time rather than measuring the absorption of X-rays, the equipment measures the emission of positrons from different parts of the brain.

The more metabolically active the brain cells are, the more they are respiring, and so the more 2-deoxyglucose they take up. A volunteer who has been given labelled 2-deoxyglucose lies in the scanner, and is then given a particular stimulation, or asked to think about a particular thing. The PET scan picks up which parts of the brain emit the most positrons, indicating that they are metabolically active during these processes. *Figure 4.10* shows one example of the results of such an investigation.

Magnetic resonance imaging, or **MRI**, can also be used to pinpoint which parts of the brain are active under different circumstances. The subject lies with their head surrounded by a huge magnet, and computer-controlled equipment measures the magnetic field in different parts of the brain. Haemoglobin has a small effect on magnetic fields, because it contains iron. When it is combined with oxygen, in the form of oxyhaemoglobin, this magnetic effect is much smaller than when it is in the form of deoxyhaemoglobin. So differences in the magnetic effects detected in different parts of the brain can indicate where most haemoglobin is oxygenated, and where most is deoxygenated. Areas where the brain cells are most active have a greater rate of blood flow to them, with a higher proportion of oxygenated haemoglobin.

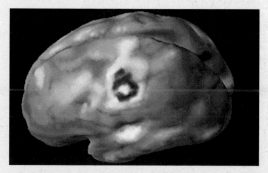

● **Figure 4.10** A PET scan of the left–hand side of a human brain, as the person carries out an exercise involving the fingers of the right hand. The red and white areas show where glucose consumption is highest, in this case in the motor area in the cerebral cortex.

can show which parts of the brain are used during particular activities. Some of the various types of brain scans are described in *box 4A* (page 55).

We would very much like to be able to understand human behaviour in terms of the physiological processes that take place in the brain. We have gone a little way towards being able to do this – we know that some particular parts of the brain control specific processes, and we know a little about the nature, distribution and effects of the many different neurotransmitters that are found in the brain. Many physiologists, however, believe that the sheer complexity of the almost infinite number of possible interconnections between the huge number of neurones in the brain means that we will never be able to describe their interactions, and the resulting behaviour, precisely.

The structure of the brain

Figure 4.11 shows the gross structure of the human brain. The functions of the major parts of the brain are summarised in *table 4.2*.

If you could 'unfold' the human brain, you would see that it is really just a very expanded extension of the spinal cord. It contains ventricles filled with **cerebro-spinal fluid**, which are continuous with the fluid in the spinal cord. The brain and spinal cord themselves are made up of neurones – some myelinated and some not.

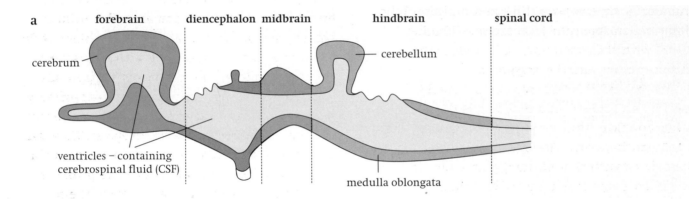

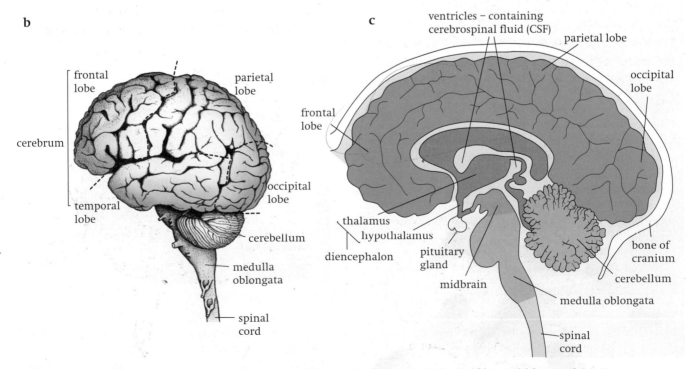

● **Figure 4.11 a** The basic structure of a mammalian brain, as it might look if it could be 'unfolded'.
b External structure of the human brain. **c** Vertical section through the human brain.

Areas where most of the neurones are myelinated look white, while areas where most of the neurones are unmyelinated look grey.

By far the largest part of the human brain is the **cerebrum**, which is divided into left and right **cerebral hemispheres**. They are linked by an area of tissue called the **corpus callosum**. The cerebral hemispheres of humans are so large that they have come to lie over much of the rest of the brain. The surface of each cerebral hemisphere is covered by a highly folded layer of tissue called the **cerebral cortex**. Although the details of all the small folds do vary between individuals, some of the larger ones are always in the same position, and the parts of the cerebral cortex between these folds have been given different names. These are the **frontal lobe**, **parietal lobe**, **temporal lobe** and **occipital lobe**. Deep within the cerebrum are several other areas with their own names, including the **hippocampus** and the **amygdala**.

Just behind the cerebrum in an 'unfolded' brain, and below it in a real one, is the **diencephalon**. This contains the **thalamus** and the **hypothalamus**. The hypothalamus is closely associated with the pituitary gland, but the pituitary gland is not part of the brain.

Behind and beneath the thalamus lies the small area known as the **midbrain**, and above this is the cerebellum. The **cerebellum**, like the cerebrum, has a folded surface and is divided into several lobes. Beneath it is the **medulla oblongata**, which merges into the spinal cord.

Part of brain	Function
cerebrum	all higher-order processes, including thinking, language, emotions, planning, memory
hypothalamus	control of the autonomic nervous system; control of some endocrine glands
cerebellum	control and coordination of movement and posture
medulla oblongata	control of breathing movements, heart rate, action of smooth muscle in the alimentary canal

● **Table 4.2** Summary of the functions of the major parts of the brain.

Functions of the cerebrum

The cerebrum is the part of the brain responsible for all the 'higher-order' processes, such as thinking, language, memory and emotions. Its large size in humans indicates how important these processes are in us, compared with other species of animals.

The cerebral cortex of both cerebral hemispheres receives sensory information from many different sense organs, such as eyes and ears, and processes this information. Areas which receive this information are called sensory areas. The two hemispheres receive information from the opposite sides of the body – the right hemisphere receives information from the left side, and the left hemisphere receives it from the right side. The parts of the cerebral cortex that first receive this information are called **primary sensory areas**, and you can see the positions of the primary sensory areas dealing with inputs from the ears (auditory) and eyes (visual) in *figure 4.12*.

Other areas receive impulses from the primary sensory areas, and integrate information coming in from the different types of receptors. These are known as **association areas**, and they make up a great deal of the cerebral cortex in all primates, including ourselves. There are three of them, which you can see in *figure 4.12*. A large association area in the parietal, temporal and

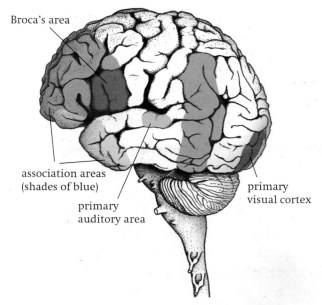

● **Figure 4.12** Some important areas of the cerebral cortex.

occipital lobes is involved in producing our perceptions resulting from what our eyes see, ears hear and other sense organs tell us about the position of different parts of our body. Another association area in the frontal lobe, called the prefrontal association complex, is involved in planning actions and movements. The third association area, known as the limbic association area, is concerned with emotions and memory.

The association areas of the left hemisphere, especially the parietal–temporal–occipital complex, are also responsible for our understanding and use of language. We have already seen that one small area, called Broca's area, has long been known to be involved in the *production* of language in speech or in writing. Later, in 1876, the German neurologist Carl Wernicke found a different area to be responsible for the *understanding* of language. PET scans of active brains show the picture to be even more complex than this, with different parts of the cerebral cortex being involved in looking at, listening to, speaking or thinking about words (*figure 4.13*). This is a good example of how the different areas of the cerebral cortex must interact to carry out even the simplest of thoughts or actions.

The parietal lobe of the right hemisphere, however, is more concerned with non-verbal processes, such as being able to visualise objects in three dimensions, and in recognising faces. This asymmetrical distribution of the sites for language and 3D processing in the brain has fascinated many people, not only neurologists, and a number of rather speculative ideas have developed from it. Some of these are described in *box 4B*.

Functions of the hypothalamus

The hypothalamus receives a wide range of information about the body, in the form of nerve impulses from many parts of the brain. It integrates this information, and then brings about responses either through the autonomic nervous system, or through the secretions of the pituitary gland.

One example of this is the control of body temperature, which involves the autonomic

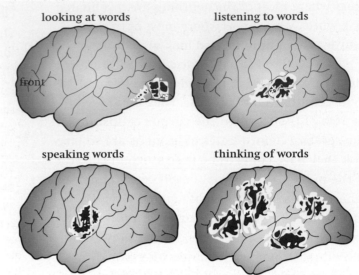

looking at words   listening to words   speaking words   thinking of words

- **Figure 4.13** Drawings made from PET scans of the human brain whle looking at, listening to, speaking and thinking of words. Yellow areas have quite high activity, red have high activity and white have the highest level of activity. Green areas are relatively inactive.

nervous system. The hypothalamus receives information about skin temperature in different parts of the body from sensory neurones carrying impulses from temperature receptors in the skin, and also from receptors inside the hypothalamus itself, which measure the temperature of the blood. All this information is integrated in the hypothalamus, and then impulses are sent through the neurones of the autonomic nervous system to bring about appropriate responses, such as shivering if too cold, or sweating if too hot.

The hypothalamus also helps to control the secretion of hormones from endocrine glands. It is directly connected to the **pituitary gland**, which lies just beneath it. The secretions of the anterior and posterior parts of the pituitary gland are controlled in different ways.

Secretions from the **posterior pituitary gland** are controlled by neurones running from the hypothalamus into the pituitary (*figure 4.14a*, see page 60). The role of these neurones is unusual. Rather than secreting a neurotransmitter to pass on an impulse to another neurone, they actually secrete the hormones themselves. These hormones are formed in the hypothalamus, and then carried along the neurones to their endings. When impulses arrive along the neurones, the hormones

Box 4B The right and left cerebral hemispheres

In the mid-1960s, some experiments were carried out to investigate the perception and behaviour of people who had lost the connection between the right and left cerebral hemispheres - the corpus callosum. This loss was the result of an operation to reduce the severity of epileptic fits that they had been suffering.

One such experiment involved showing the person an object in such a way that it could only be seen by one eye. If it was the right eye that saw the object, the person had no problem in naming it. However, if it was seen with the left eye, the person was not able to give its name, although he could pick out other objects like it when allowed to feel them through a cloth.

The explanation for these results involves the difference between the left and right hemispheres. Impulses from the right eye are taken to the left cerebral hemisphere, which is the one known to be involved in language. So something seen with the right eye can be named. However, when the object is seen with the left eye, impulses pass only to the right hemisphere, and in this case the person's brain cannot produce language to describe it. In people with the corpus callosum intact, it is possible for messages to be passed from one side of the brain to the other, so even if the object is seen only with the left eye, the left side of the brain still receives information about it and the object can be named.

Further experiments of this type have confirmed that, in most people, the left hemisphere is the one which is specialised to understand and produce language. In these people, the right hemisphere has only a very small ability to deal with language, and is specialised to deal with spatial perception. In general, it seems that the left hemisphere is better at tasks which involve logical, *sequential* analysis, while the right hemisphere is better at tasks that involve *simultaneous* processing of many different inputs. An example could be recognition of a face, where our right cerebral hemisphere deals with the sum of all the information about the shapes, sizes and positions of all the different components of the face. Language is not involved in such recognition.

Each hemisphere appears to be perfectly capable of taking on either type of task, so long as this develops during the early years of life. In children with damage to their left hemisphere, language frequently develops normally, because the right hemisphere gradually takes over its control. This does not happen in adults, however, showing that once the hemispheres have become specialised it is difficult for them to change their roles.

Interestingly, not everyone's left and right hemispheres fit this pattern. Around 4% of right-handed people show the opposite arrangement – their right hemisphere deals with language, and the left with spatial problems. This percentage is much greater in left-handed people, of whom 15% show this unusual arrangement. Moreover, in another 15% of left-handed people, *both* hemispheres are involved in the control of language.

There is also some evidence that the functions of the right and left hemispheres differ in males and females. One series of experiments involved asking children to touch and manipulate two different objects, without being able to see them. They were then asked to identify the objects from pictures. Identifying the objects by touch would be expected to be dealt with in the right hemisphere, which would suggest that it should be easier to do if the objects were felt with the left hand (i.e. the one which sends information to the right hemisphere). This was found to be so in most boys from the age of six upwards. Girls, however, showed no difference between the left and right hemispheres until the age of 13. This suggests that perhaps boys develop the specialisation of right and left hemispheres at an earlier age than girls.

Further evidence from experiments carried out with adults suggests that, in general, adult female brains show less difference between the functions of the left and right hemispheres than do those of men. And some investigations have produced results suggesting that women do better than men on 'left hemisphere' tasks involving skills such as language or arithmetical calculations, while men do better than women on 'right hemisphere' tasks involving spatial relationships and complex mathematical problems involving reasoning. However, these results are only averages applying to groups of people, and there are many women who are excellent at spatial tasks or complex mathematics, and men who have excellent verbal skills. Moreover, brain functions are affected by far more than anatomy and fundamental physiology – they are also hugely affected by our environment, especially our experiences as we grow from children to adults.

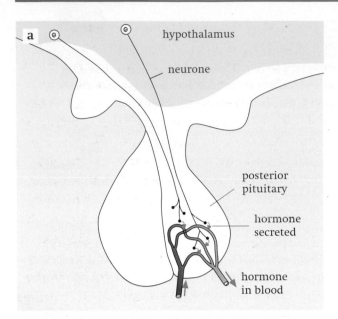
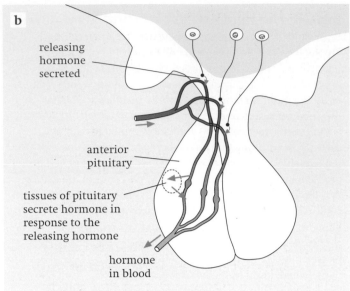

● **Figure 4.14** Structural and functional relationship between the hypothalamus and the pituitary gland. **a** Posterior pituitary secretion. **b** Anterior pituitary secretion.

are released from their endings in a similar way to the release of a neurotransmitter, and pass into the blood. The two hormones produced and released in this way are **antidiuretic hormone** or ADH, which controls water reabsorption in the kidneys, and **oxytocin**, which is involved in contraction of the uterus during birth, and ejection of milk from the mammary glands during lactation.

Secretions from the **anterior pituitary gland** have a different method of production and release (*figure 4.14b*). Neurones in the hypothalamus produce several different hormones, and secrete these into the surrounding blood vessels. This is an example of **neurosecretion** – secretion of substances from neurones. The hormones are carried through the blood vessels into the anterior pituitary gland, where they affect the production and release of a variety of other hormones produced in the pituitary itself. The hormones from the hypothalamus are called **releasing hormones** if they stimulate this, and **inhibiting hormones** if they inhibit it. *Table 4.3* gives some examples of these hormones and their effects.

Action of hypothalamus	Effect on pituitary	Result
secretion of thyrotropin releasing hormone	release of thyroid-stimulating hormone from anterior pituitary	release of thyroxine from the thyroid gland, which increases rate of metabolism
secretion of growth hormone releasing hormone	release of growth hormone from anterior pituitary	growth of cells and tissues
secretion of gonadotrophin releasing hormone	release of luteinising hormone (LH) and follicle-stimulating hormone (FSH) from anterior pituitary	FSH causes growth of follicles in ovary and stimulates sperm production in testis; LH helps to cause ovulation and stimulates the secretion of oestrogen, progesterone and testosterone
production of antidiuretic hormone (ADH)	ADH is released from nerve endings in the posterior pituitary	increases reabsorption of water from the collecting duct, resulting in excretion of small amounts of concentrated urine
production of oxytocin	oxytocin is released from nerve endings in the posterior pituitary	contraction of uterus during birth; ejection of milk from mammary glands during lactation

● **Table 4.3** Some effects of the hypothalamus on the endocrine system.

Functions of the cerebellum

The cerebellum is concerned with the control and coordination of movement and posture. It receives inputs from all other parts of the central nervous system, and also directly from sensory neurones. This information is integrated, and then impulses are sent on to other parts of the brain, especially the motor centres of the cerebellum. Some neurologists suggest that the cerebellum helps to compensate for small errors in movement, by comparing the intended movement (indicated by impulses arising in the cerebrum) with what is actually happening (indicated by impulses coming in from sense organs). It also appears to be involved in the learning of tasks requiring carefully coordinated movements, such as riding a bicycle, playing a musical instrument or catching a ball.

SAQ 4.5

The size of the cerebellum compared with the rest of the brain varies considerably in different groups of animals. For example, it tends to be relatively large in fish and birds, and relatively small in reptiles. With reference to the lifestyles of these groups, and the functions of the cerebellum, suggest why this is so.

Functions of the medulla oblongata

The medulla oblongata is responsible for the control of breathing, heart rate and blood pressure.

Groups of neurones in the medulla oblongata produce rhythmic patterns of impulses, which pass along the vagus nerve (part of the autonomic nervous system) to the muscles of the diaphragm and the intercostal muscles. This causes the muscles to contract and relax regularly. Impulses from the cerebrum to the medulla oblongata can modify this pattern, so that you can consciously control your breathing pattern. The pattern is also modified by changes in the carbon dioxide concentration in the blood. If this rises, it is detected by receptor cells in the medulla oblongata, and also in the walls of the carotid arteries and aorta. The neurones in the medulla oblongata respond to this by increasing the frequency of impulses sent to the breathing muscles, resulting in faster and deeper breathing movements.

A different part of the medulla oblongata, though closely connected to the breathing centres, contains groups of neurones that are responsible for regulating heart rate and blood pressure. They receive information about blood pressure from baroreceptors (pressure receptors) in the walls of the carotid arteries, and information about the concentration of carbon dioxide from the receptors described above. Both sympathetic and parasympathetic neurones can carry impulses from the medulla oblongata to the sino-atrial node in the right atrium of the heart, which acts as the pacemaker. If blood pressure is low, or if there is too much carbon dioxide in the blood, then the medulla oblongata sends impulses along neurones that are part of the sympathetic system, and this causes the SAN to beat faster. High blood pressure or low carbon dioxide concentration cause impulses to be sent along the vagus nerve (part of the parasympathetic nervous system), causing the SAN to beat more slowly.

Alzheimer's disease

Around 750 000 people in the UK suffer from some form of **dementia**. Dementia is a general reduction and loss in mental abilities such as memory, logical thinking and language. Of these people, approximately half have the form of dementia known as Alzheimer's disease.

The symptoms of Alzheimer's disease

Alzheimer's disease gets its name from Alois Alzheimer, a German psychiatrist. He studied the brain of a woman who died in 1906, following several years during which she had progressively lost her memory and become increasingly confused. Alzheimer found that the tissue of some parts of her cerebral cortex looked very abnormal. Some of the neurones had bundles of fibres in them, which he called 'tangles', whilst in between the neurones there were dark-staining deposits that were not present in a normal brain. He called these deposits 'plaques' (*figure 4.15* overleaf).

Neither tangles nor plaques show up on any of the types of brain scan that are currently available. It is therefore not possible to make a definite diagnosis of Alzheimer's disease in a person until

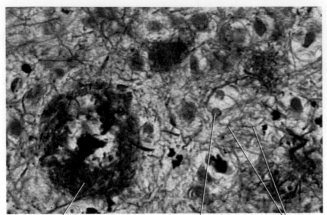

amyloid fibrils
in a plaque

cell body of
a neurone

dendrites
and axons

● **Figure 4.15** Light micrograph of tissue from the brain of a man who had Alzheimer's disease (× 400). The dark areas are plaques and tangles.

after death, when the structure of their cerebral cortex can be investigated. CAT or MRI scans (*box 4A*) do, however, show a reduction in size of the brain in patients with Alzheimer's disease. Normally, though, the diagnosis is done purely by looking at the changing pattern of behaviour of the patient, and it is not always possible to be certain whether this is due to Alzheimer's disease or some other form of dementia.

The symptoms usually begin with an increasing loss of memory. The person becomes more and more forgetful, especially of recent events. So, for example, they may say the same thing or ask the same question repeatedly during a conversation. It becomes more and more difficult for them to concentrate on anything. Anxiety increases, and there may be considerable personality changes – for example, the person may become aggressive or depressed. They may have hallucinations, or imagine that they are being persecuted by someone. Eventually they may lose the ability to identify people, even their close family. These personality changes put a great strain on family members who are attempting to care for them.

The causes of Alzheimer's disease

We still do not know what causes Alzheimer's disease. We do not know exactly what makes the tangles and plaques form in the brain, nor even if these are *causing* the symptoms, or are just a result of some other change in the brain that causes

both the symptoms of Alzheimer's and the development of tangles and plaques. We do know that the tangles in the neurones are made of a protein called **tau**, and that as tau builds up in the neurones they die. And we know that the plaques contain a peptide known as **beta amyloid**, **Aβ**.

Aβ is made from a larger protein molecule called beta amyloid precursor protein, or **APP**. APP is a protein found in the plasma membranes of all mammalian cells, although it is not yet known what its function is. Some APP is converted into Aβ by an enzyme that cuts off the part of the APP molecule that protrudes from the outer surface of the plasma membrane, releasing the Aβ into the tissue fluid outside the cells. This is a normal event, and Aβ is secreted by normal cells throughout life. It appears that the plaques of Aβ form in the cerebral cortex when much more Aβ is secreted than normal, or when the Aβ is made up of a chain of 42 amino acids rather than the usual 40. So, is abnormal metabolism of APP the root cause of Alzheimer's disease?

A clue can be found by looking at the tiny proportion of people with Alzheimer's who have what is called 'familial' Alzheimer's disease, in which the disease is inherited. People with inherited Alzheimer's tend to develop it relatively early in life, between the ages of 35 and 60. Some forms of familial Alzheimer's are caused by different alleles of the gene that codes for APP, while others are caused by different alleles for the enzymes that act on APP to form Aβ. People suffering from inherited Alzheimer's have increased levels of Aβ42. So it does look as though the cause of inherited Alzheimer's is something to do with the metabolism of APP.

However, in the vast majority of people with Alzheimer's disease, there is no evidence of a purely genetic cause. But there *is* evidence for the involvement of genes that code for another protein, called apolipoprotein E, or **APOe**. About half of all people with Alzheimer's have a particular allele of the gene, called ε4, that codes for APOe, and there is some evidence that the presence of this allele may increase the rate at which Aβ is deposited in plaques. At the moment we do not understand how APOe could influence the develoment of plaques or tangles, though some research suggests that it may be involved in helping neurones to recover after injury. Thus, it may be that the type of APOe coded for by ε4 is less effective at this than other types.

Not everyone who has the ε4 allele develops Alzheimer's. So, although the allele increases the risk of getting the disease, some other environmental factors must also be influencing this. Ageing is one of these factors. Less than 1 person in 1000 under the age of 65 has Alzheimer's, whilst 1 in 20 over the age of 65 have it, showing that the risk of getting it increases with age. However, these figures also show that 9 out of 10 people over 65 do not get Alzheimer's, so obviously ageing alone is not the cause. Other possible environmental factors include the use that is made of the brain throughout life. For example, some studies suggest that people who lead varied and active lives are less likely to get Alzheimer's. Severe blows to the head, especially if these happen to someone over the age of 50, may increase the risk of getting Alzheimer's. There is also evidence that risk factors for coronary heart disease, such as smoking and high cholesterol levels, may also be risk factors for Alzheimer's. However, the results from all of these studies are inconclusive, and the importance of all of these possible risk factors is controversial.

We do not know how the visible changes in the brain cause the symptoms of Alzheimer's. Certainly the cells in the regions of the brain that are affected by the plaques and tangles are known to secrete less of the neurotransmitter acetylcholine. Clearly, as the changes are in the cerebral cortex, the part of the brain that is responsible for all higher-order processes (page 57), it is not surprising that the symptoms involve memory, language and emotions.

Preventing and treating Alzheimer's disease

Currently, we can neither prevent nor treat Alzheimer's. There are drugs that can temporarily reduce some of the symptoms, but nothing that can genuinely halt the progress of the disease. For example, drugs that inhibit acetylcholinesterase (the enzyme that breaks down acetylcholine at synapses) can help for a while, by slowing down the rate at which levels of acetylcholine decline in the affected parts of the brain. This has a short-term beneficial effect on memory, but does nothing to stop the development of the disease in the long term.

Much research is being carried out to try to find drugs that could be used to treat the disease. This is really difficult to do, however, when we do not fully understand what is causing it. For example, some pharmaceutical companies are trying to develop inhibitors of the enzymes that cleave APP to produce Aβ, but as these enzymes have not yet been identified this is a very difficult task. Recently, a vaccine has been developed which, when introduced into the brains of mice bred to develop Alzheimer's, seems to break down the plaques of beta amyloid. Whether this could ever work in humans, or whether even if it did, it would halt or reverse the development of the disease, is not yet known.

In the meantime, the best that we can do to reduce the chances of developing Alzheimer's disease is to make sure that we use our brains regularly for a variety of different things (such as studying for examinations, learning to ice skate, doing crossword puzzles), avoid blows to the head (so taking up boxing is not a good idea) and following the same rules as those for avoiding heart disease – a good diet and plenty of exercise.

SUMMARY

- The human nervous system is made up of the central nervous system (brain and spinal cord) and the peripheral nervous system. The peripheral nervous system can be divided structurally and functionally into the somatic system, which involves all sensory neurones and also motor neurones serving skeletal muscles, and the autonomic nervous system.

- The autonomic nervous system can itself be divided into the sympathetic system, which prepares the body for 'fight or flight' and the parasympathetic system which helps it to 'rest and digest'. Neurones of the sympathetic system often use noradrenaline as a neurotransmitter, while those of the parasympathetic system use acetylcholine.

- The largest part of the human brain is the cerebrum, made up of two cerebral hemispheres each with an outer, folded layer called the cerebral cortex. It is responsible for language, thought, planning and emotions. In most people, the left hemisphere is responsible for language, and the right for spatial recognition and manipulation.

- The hypothalamus is closely associated with the pituitary gland (which is not part of the brain), and controls its secretions. Hormones secreted from the posterior pituitary gland are made in the hypothalamus and travel

down to the pituitary along nerve axons. Hormones secreted from the anterior pituitary gland are made in the pituitary, and released in response to releasing hormones made in the hypothalamus. The hypothalamus also acts via the autonomic nervous system, for example by integrating information about body temperature and then sending impulses through the autonomic system to bring about appropriate actions to keep temperature constant.

- The cerebellum is responsible for control and coordination of movement and posture.

- The medulla oblongata controls breathing rate, heart rate and blood pressure.

- Alzheimer's disease is a type of dementia, which develops in about 5% of people over the age of 65. It is characterised by the formation of plaques of beta amyloid protein between neurones in the cerebral cortex, and tangles of tau protein inside neurones. The causes of this are not yet known. People with Alzheimer's become increasingly forgetful, especially of recent events, lose their ability to think logically and to recognise familiar objects including people, and may show personality changes. As yet, there is no treatment that can cure, or slow the progress of, Alzheimer's disease.

Questions

1 Explain the differences between each of the following:
   a the cerebrum and the cerebellum;
   b the somatic nervous system and the autonomic nervous system;
   c the effects of the parasympathetic and the sympathetic nervous systems on the digestive system.

2 a Outline the functions of the cerebrum in the human brain.

   b Describe the changes that occur in the cerebrum of a person with Alzheimer's disease, and discuss the possible causes of this disease.

3 a Describe the effects of the parasympathetic and sympathetic nervous systems in the control of heart action.

   b What role does the medulla oblongata play in this control?

CHAPTER 5

Sense organs and the reception of stimuli

By the end of this chapter you should be able to:

1 describe the gross structure of the eye and outline the functions of its parts, including accommodation;

2 describe the structure of the retina with reference to the arrangement of rods, cones, bipolar cells and ganglion cells;

3 relate the structure of the eye to visual acuity, colour vision and sensitivity to different light intensities;

4 outline the general principles involved in the reception and recognition of visual stimuli by the brain;

5 discuss the effects of ageing on the eye, with reference to cataracts and their treatment;

6 describe the gross structure of the ear and outline the functions of its parts in hearing and balance.

Many of our actions are responses to what is happening around us. We have several different kinds of **sense organs**, which contain **receptor cells** that are sensitive to particular features of the environment. Receptor cells are able to absorb different types of energy from the environment and transfer this energy into changes in electrical potential across the plasma membranes of neurones. *Table 5.1* overleaf lists some of the different types of receptor cells in the human body.

In this chapter, we will look at the structure and function of two sense organs – the eye and ear. Sight is arguably the most important sense for humans – most of our perception of the world around us, and our memories of it, are based on sight – and therefore we will consider the way in which we receive and perceive visual images in some detail.

How the eye focuses light

Figures 5.1 and *5.2* overleaf show the gross structure of the human eye. The part which contains the receptor cells is the **retina**. Most of the other parts of the eye are concerned with focusing light onto the retina, or with protection.

The structure of the eye

In all parts of the eye except the front, the outer layer is the **sclera**, a very tough, white, connective tissue layer which protects the structures within it. The sclera helps to maintain the shape of the eye, as the pressure of the **vitreous humour** pushes out on it, and the sclera resists this pressure.

The tissue next to the sclera is the **choroid layer**, which is richly suppled with blood vessels. The inner part of the choroid is made up of a layer of cells containing the dark pigment

Table 5.1 Some examples of energy conversions by receptors. Each type of receptor converts a particular form of energy into electrical energy – that is, a nerve impulse.

Receptor	Sense	Form in which energy is received
rod or cone cells in retina	sight	light
taste buds on tongue	taste	chemical potential
olfactory cells in nose	smell	chemical potential
Pacinian corpuscles in skin	pressure	movement and pressure
Meissner's corpuscles in skin	touch	movement and pressure
Ruffini's endings in skin	temperature	heat
proprioceptors (stretch receptors) in muscles	placement of limbs	mechanical displacement – stretching
hair cells in semicircular canals in ear	balance	movement
hair cells in cochlea	hearing	sound

melanin, called the **pigmented epithelium**.

The innermost layer is the **retina**, which contains several different types of cells including the receptor cells themselves – the **rods** and **cones**. We will look at the structure of the retina in more detail on pages 69–71. Axons of cells in the retina leave the back of the eye in the **optic nerve**.

At the front of the eye, the outer covering is a thin layer of protective cells known as the **conjunctiva**, covered by a film of fluid secreted from the **tear ducts**. Beneath this lies a thick, transparent layer – the **cornea** – which is continuous with the sclera, and which plays a major part in focusing light rays onto the retina. The **iris** is a circular tissue containing pigmented cells, which helps to control the amount of light passing through onto the retina. The size of the circular space in the centre of the iris, the **pupil**, is varied by contraction and relaxation of the circular and radial muscles in the iris (page 54).

The **ciliary body** contains **ciliary muscles** which, as we will see, help to control the shape of the lens. The **lens** is made of stacks of long, narrow, transparent cells. It is biconvex (that is, it curves outwards on both sides), and is about 4 mm thick. It is held in position by

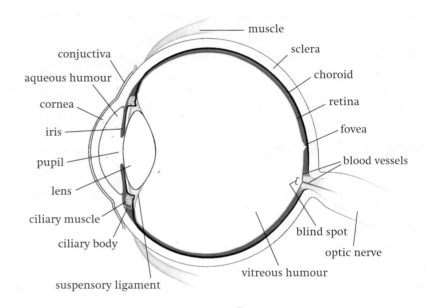

● **Figure 5.1** The structure of a human eye.

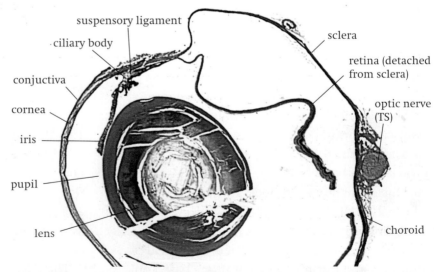

● **Figure 5.2** Light micrograph of a section through an eye (× 6). During the process of cutting the section and staining it, the retina has come away from the choroid and sclera, and the suspensory ligaments are no longer supporting the lens.

the **suspensory ligaments**, which run between the lens and the ciliary body.

The retina is well supplied with blood capillaries, but the conjunctiva, cornea, and lens do not contain blood vessels. The conjunctiva is bathed by fluid from the tear ducts, while the cornea and lens obtain their oxygen and nutrients from the two fluids contained within the eye – the **aqueous humour** and the **vitreous humour**. 'Aqueous' means watery, and 'vitreous' means 'glassy', and these names refer to the fact that the aqueous humour is much less viscous than the vitreous humour. The two humours also help to maintain the shape of the eye, by exerting outward pressure on the tissues which surround them.

SAQ 5.1

Suggest why it is important that the conjunctiva, cornea and lens do not have blood vessels in them.

Focusing and accommodation

In order for a clear image to be perceived, light rays must be focused onto the retina. The most sensitive part of the retina is the **fovea**, and when you look directly at an object this is the part of the retina on which the image is formed. The image that is formed is upside down. However, the brain deals with this image so that we perceive it

as being the right way up; this is part of the complex processing of the visual image that takes place in the brain, described on pages 74–5.

Figure 5.3a shows how light rays from a distant object are brought to a focus on the fovea. These light rays are parallel to each other. They are **refracted** (bent) inwards as they pass through the cornea, aqueous humour, lens and vitreous humour. The majority of this refraction happens at the surface of the cornea – not, as you may think, at the lens.

The function of the lens is to make fine adjustments to the refraction of the light rays, so that light rays arriving from various distances can be brought to a sharp focus on the retina. Whereas light rays from distant objects are parallel to each other when they reach the eye, light rays from closer objects are diverging. The closer the object is, the greater the divergence of the light rays, and the more they need to be refracted inwards to be brought to a focus. This is achieved by making the lens thicker and more convex, so that the light rays are bent sharply as they pass through it (*figure 5.3b*).

The change in shape of the lens, in order to focus on objects at a particular distance from the eye, is known as **accommodation**. It is achieved by varying the tension on the suspensory ligaments which hold the lens in position. When this

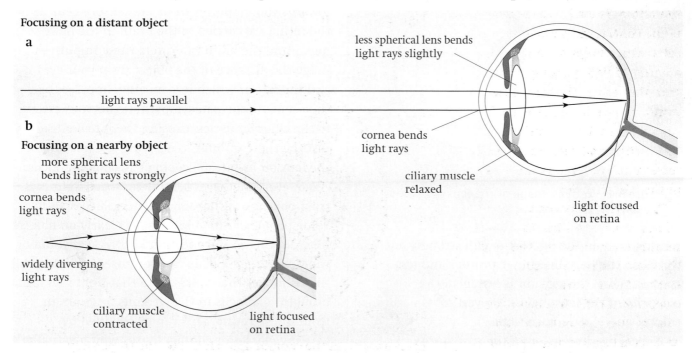

Focusing on a distant object

a

light rays parallel

less spherical lens bends light rays slightly

cornea bends light rays

ciliary muscle relaxed

light focused on retina

b

Focusing on a nearby object

more spherical lens bends light rays strongly

cornea bends light rays

widely diverging light rays

ciliary muscle contracted

light focused on retina

● **Figure 5.3** Focusing on **a** distant and **b** near objects.

The contents of the eye are under pressure

1   Water uptake keeps the aqueous and vitreous humours under pressure.

2   The aqueous and vitreous humours push outward producing tension in the sclera.

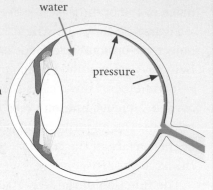

How the lens is made less spherical

1   The ciliary muscle relaxes.

2   The tension in the sclera pulls on the relaxed ring of muscle, and this in turn pulls on the suspensory ligaments.

3   The suspensory ligaments stretch the lens which becomes thin (less convex).

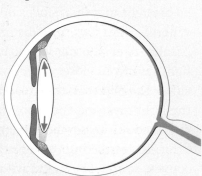

How the lens becomes more spherical

1   The ciliary muscle contracts, reducing its diameter and so loosening the tension on the suspensory ligaments.

2   The lens becomes partially isolated from the tension in the sclera, and is allowed to form its natural shape. The natural shape of the lens is nearly spherical.

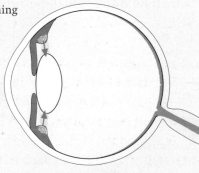

● **Figure 5.4** How the shape of the lens is altered.

tension is high, the ligaments pull strongly outwards on the lens, making it thinner and less convex. When the tension is lessened, the elasticity of the lens makes it revert to its natural, thicker and more convex state.

The change in tension of the suspensory ligaments is brought about by the actions of the ciliary muscles (*figure 5.4*). These are smooth muscles, under the control of the autonomic nervous system (page 51). The ciliary body is joined to the tough sclera, which is constantly being pushed outwards by the pressure of the aqueous and vitreous humours, and which therefore pulls outwards on the ciliary muscles. When the circular ciliary muscles are relaxed, the sclera pulls the circle out wide, and this in turn exerts tension on the suspensory ligaments. When the ciliary muscles are contracted, the diameter of the circle decreases, and tension on the suspensory ligaments is lessened.

From this description, you can see that the resting condition of the eye – that is, when the ciliary muscles are relaxed – produces high tension on the suspensory ligaments. This means that the lens is pulled outwards, becoming thinner and less convex. In this state, the eye is focused on distant objects. However, as you read these words your ciliary muscles are contracted, releasing the tension on the suspensory ligaments so that the lens is thick and more convex. Some people find that prolonged focusing on near objects makes their eyes tired, because it involves prolonged contraction of the ciliary muscles.

The adjustment of the shape of the lens is an example of a reflex action. Imagine, for example, that you are watching an object that is moving towards you. Impulses from the sensory cells in the retina are carried to the brain in the optic nerve, and the brain interprets these impulses to judge the distance of the object from your eyes and the rate at which it is moving. Impulses are then sent via the parasympathetic nervous system to the ciliary muscles, causing them to contract by just the right amount to decrease the tension on the lens bit by bit, so keeping the object in focus.

Not everyone's eyes are able to focus light rays from objects at different distances successfully. Some people are unable to focus clearly on objects far from the eye, a condition known as **myopia** or short-sightedness. This can be caused by an eyeball that is longer than normal, so that light rays are brought to a focus in the vitreous humour, in front of the retina. This can be rectified by wearing glasses or contact lenses which actually *diverge* the light rays before they reach the cornea, so that by the time the cornea and lens have bent them inwards again the image focuses precisely onto the retina.

Other people can focus perfectly on distant objects, but not on ones close to the eye. This condition is known as **hypermetropia**, or long-sightedness, and results from the light rays not being bent inwards sufficiently to have arrived at a focus by the time they reach the retina. It is corrected by wearing converging lenses, which bend the light rays inwards before they reach the cornea and lens.

As a person ages, the ability of the lens to change shape decreases, so that it is increasingly difficult to adjust focus. It may then become necessary to have two pairs of glasses – one to help with close vision, and one for distant vision. The two different types of lenses may be combined into one pair of bifocal spectacles, in which the converging lens is at the bottom and the diverging lens at the top.

SAQ 5.2 _____

Explain why the lenses in bifocal spectacles are arranged in this way.

The retina

The retina is the part of the eye that is sensitive to light. It is here that energy in light rays is converted to energy in nerve impulses (action potentials) that are carried along the optic nerve to the brain.

The structure of the retina

Figure 5.5 shows the structure of the retina. It contains two different types of photoreceptor cells, **rods** and **cones**. These cells are precisely arranged in a single layer, with one end making close contact with the pigmented epithelium just outside them. This epithelium absorbs any light that passes through the layer of rods and cones, so that it is not reflected back into the eye; if it was, it would reduce the clarity of the image that we see.

The retina contains other layers of cells, including special types of neurones known as **bipolar cells** and **ganglion cells**. These are

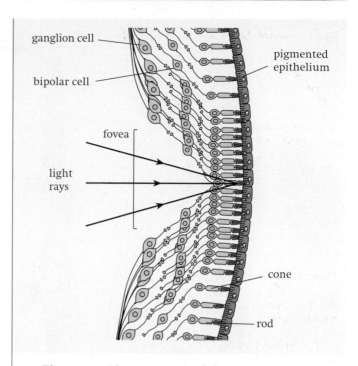

● **Figure 5.5** The structure of the retina.

responsible for conveying information from the rods and cones to the optic nerve. You may be surprised to realise that light has to pass *through* these cell layers before it reaches the rods and cones behind them. The neurones in these layers are not myelinated, making the layers relatively transparent. Moreover, in the area right in the middle of the fovea, the cell bodies of these neurones, and blood vessels that supply the retina, are shifted to the side, so that light reaches the photoreceptors in this region without having to pass through other cell layers first.

The part of the retina from which the optic nerve arises is sometimes known as the **optic disc**. There are no photoreceptor cells here, so light falling onto this region cannot be seen. This gives the optic disc its other name – the **blind spot**. Usually, we do not notice this, because if light from an object is falling onto the blind spot in one eye, it cannot also fall onto the blind spot in the other eye.

The structure of rods and cones

Rod cells and cone cells (*figure 5.6* overleaf) have very similar structures. The part of the cell closest to the outside of the eye is known as the **outer segment**, and the part closest to the inside of the eye is the **inner segment**. The end of the inner

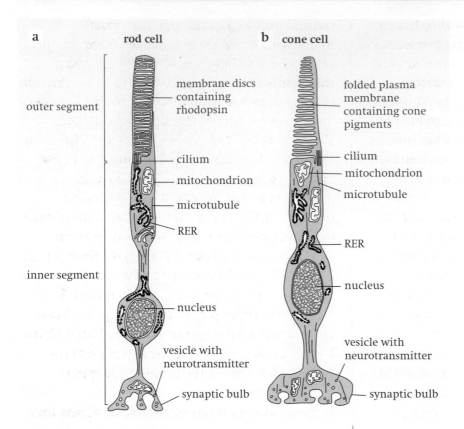

a rod cell

outer segment
- membrane discs containing rhodopsin
- cilium
- mitochondrion
- microtubule
- RER

inner segment
- nucleus
- vesicle with neurotransmitter
- synaptic bulb

b cone cell
- folded plasma membrane containing cone pigments
- cilium
- mitochondrion
- microtubule
- RER
- nucleus
- vesicle with neurotransmitter
- synaptic bulb

● **Figure 5.6** The structure of **a** a rod cell and **b** a cone cell.

segment forms synapses with the cells in the other layers of the retina.

In both rods and cones, the outer segment contains many stacks of membranes. These are formed from invaginations of the plasma membrane. In a rod cell, the invaginations pinch off from the plasma membrane, resulting in a stack of unconnected discs that lie freely in the cytoplasm. In a cone cell, however, the invaginations remain attached to the plasma membrane. The membrane discs in rod and cone cells are constantly being discarded at the tips of the cells (where they are taken in and destroyed by phagocytic cells) and renewed by the formation of new ones. In a human rod cell, about three new discs are synthesised every hour.

In both rod and cone cells, these discs provide a large surface of membrane which contains **visual pigments**. When light hits a molecule of one of these pigments, it brings about changes which may result in action potentials being

fired off along the optic nerve. In a rod cell, each pigment molecule consists of a protein called **opsin**, which lies within the membrane, to which a small light-absorbing compound called **retinal** is attached, on the outer surface. The whole molecule (opsin plus retinal) is known as **rhodopsin** (*figure 5.7*). The visual pigments in cone cells are similar, though the precise structure of the opsin part of the molecule is not the same as in rod cells. Indeed, there are three different types of opsin that are found in three different types of cone cells, and this gives us colour vision (page 72). These pigments are sometimes known as **iodopsin**, or simply as **cone pigments**. Rod cells are much more sensitive to light than cone cells, so in dim light it is our rod cells that give us most of our visual information.

The inner and outer segments of rods and cones are connected by a narrow region which contains microtubules arranged as in a cilium (*Biology 1*, page 14). The inner segment contains the nucleus and numerous mitochondria. This is where new proteins are initially formed, before passing through the connecting region into the outer segment.

Bipolar and ganglion cells

As we have seen, the inner layers of the retina contain **bipolar cells** and **ganglion cells**, both of which are types of neurones.

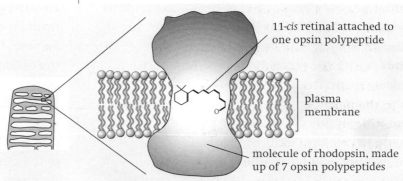

- 11-*cis* retinal attached to one opsin polypeptide
- plasma membrane
- molecule of rhodopsin, made up of 7 opsin polypeptides

● **Figure 5.7** A rhodopsin molecule in a rod cell membrane.

Bipolar cells are so named because they have a central cell body from which two sets of processes arise (*figure 5.5*). Those nearest to the layer of rods and cones are short, and branch into many endings which form synapses with either a single cone, or a number of rods. (We will consider the significance of this a little later.) The other process is longer, and forms synapses with a ganglion cell. Bipolar cells transfer information from the rods and cones to the ganglion cells.

Ganglion cells make up the inner layer of the retina. Numerous dendrites form synapses with bipolar cells, and it is here that action potentials are first generated in the retina. The action potentials pass along the axons of the ganglion cells, which make up the optic nerve, to the brain.

How a rod cell responds to light

In *Biology 2*, page 108, we saw how a neurone that is not conducing an action potential maintains a **resting potential** across its plasma membrane. The resting potential is maintained by the **sodium–potassium pump**, which constantly moves sodium ions, Na$^+$, out of the cell by active transport, and potassium ions, K$^+$, into the cell. As three sodium ions are moved out for every two potassium ions that are moved in, and as both sodium and potassium ions carry a positive charge, this results in more positive charge outside the cell than inside. The resting potential of a neurone is usually between −60 and −70 mV inside.

When no light is falling onto it, a rod cell, like a neurone, maintains a difference in electrical potential across its plasma membrane. But this potential difference has a much smaller magnitude than that of a neurone; it is normally about −40 mV inside. As in the neurone, the sodium–potassium pump constantly transports sodium ions out and potassium ions in. However, in the outer segment of the rod cell there are open channels that allow

sodium ions to pass through the plasma membrane. In the inner segment, there are open channels that allow potassium ions to pass through. So sodium ions continually flow through these channels down their concentration gradient *into* the outer segment, while potassium ions similarly flow *out* of the inner segment (*figure 5.8*). This flow of sodium and potassium ions, in the opposite direction to the way the sodium–potassium pump moves them, prevents the potential difference across the plasma membrane becoming any more than −40 mV, despite the constant activity of the sodium–potassium pump.

When light falls onto the rod cell, this situation changes. Light hitting a rhodopsin molecule causes the retinal part of it to change its shape. The normal shape (*figure 5.9*, overleaf) has a sharp kink at carbon 11, so this form is called 11-*cis*-retinal. Light causes the chain to straighten, forming all-*trans*-retinal.

The change in shape of the retinal means that it no longer fits into its binding site in opsin. This causes the whole rhodopsin molecule to change shape, into an unstable form. This in turn brings about events which cause the sodium and

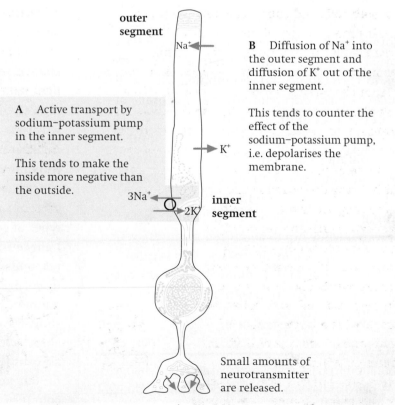

A Active transport by sodium–potassium pump in the inner segment.

This tends to make the inside more negative than the outside.

B Diffusion of Na$^+$ into the outer segment and diffusion of K$^+$ out of the inner segment.

This tends to counter the effect of the sodium–potassium pump, i.e. depolarises the membrane.

outer segment

inner segment

Small amounts of neurotransmitter are released.

● **Figure 5.8** How the membrane potential is maintained in a rod cell.

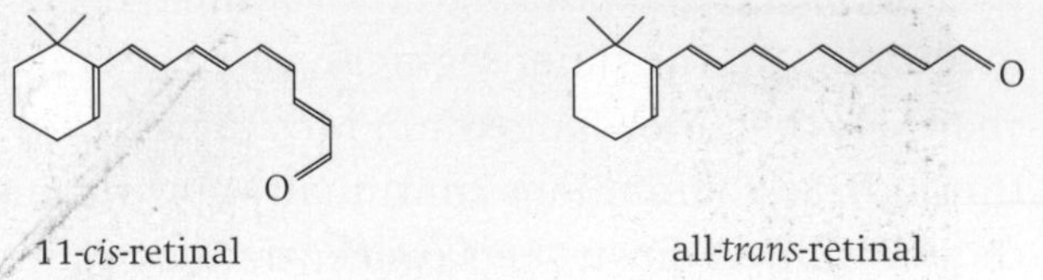

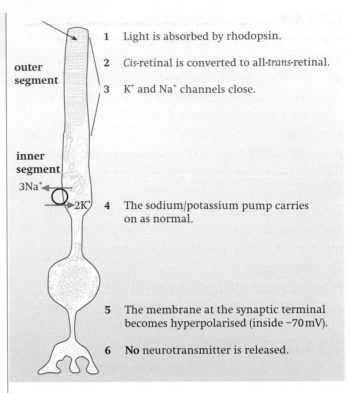

11-*cis*-retinal   all-*trans*-retinal

● **Figure 5.9** 11-*cis*-retinal and all-*trans*-retinal.

potassium channels in the plasma membrane to close (*figure 5.10*). Now sodium ions cannot diffuse back into the cell, nor potassium ions diffuse out. The sodium–potassium pump carries on working as usual, so a greater potential difference almost instantly builds up across the plasma membrane. This is −70 mV, the same as in a resting neurone. The rod cell is said to be **hyperpolarised**, which simply means that it is more polarised (has a greater potential difference across its plasma membrane) than when light is not falling on it. As we shall see, this hyperpolarisation can result in impulses being sent along the optic nerve to the brain.

The unstable form of rhodopsin that is produced when light falls onto it does not stay like that for very long. Within minutes, it breaks down into opsin and all-*trans*-retinal – though not before it has brought about the changes described above. Eventually the all-*trans*-retinal is converted back to 11-*cis*-retinal and recombined with opsin to take its place once more in the membrane of one of the discs in the rod cell.

This takes time. In bright light, most of the rhodopsin molecules break down. If you then move into dim light you have very little rhodopsin in the membranes in the rod cells, so there is nothing that can respond to the light. If, however, you wait a while (up to about ten minutes), your ability to see gradually increases. This is called **dark adaptation**, and it comes about as the opsin and all-*trans*-retinal are recombined to form rhodopsin once more.

SAQ 5.3

In addition to dark adaptation, what other change takes place in the eye, as you move from bright light into dim light?

outer segment

inner segment

3Na⁺

2K⁺

1   Light is absorbed by rhodopsin.

2   *Cis*-retinal is converted to all-*trans*-retinal.

3   K⁺ and Na⁺ channels close.

4   The sodium/potassium pump carries on as normal.

5   The membrane at the synaptic terminal becomes hyperpolarised (inside −70 mV).

6   **No** neurotransmitter is released.

● **Figure 5.10** What happens when light hits rhodopsin in a rod cell.

How cone cells respond to light

Cone cells, just like rod cells, have pigment molecules in the membranes inside the outer segment, and these pigments change their form when light falls onto them. However, whereas in a rod cell a single photon of light can be enough to bring about a response, cone cells require much more light before the pigment breaks down and causes the cell to hyperpolarize. This helps to explain why rods are so much more sensitive to light than cones are. In dim light, it is only our rods which respond to light.

Another difference between cones and rods is that, as we have seen, there are three different types of cone cells, each with a different type of light-sensitive pigment. Each of these pigments responds to a particular range of wavelengths of light (*figure 5.11*). An individual cone may contain pigment B, which is most sensitive to short-wavelength (blue) light; pigment G, which absorbs mostly green light; or pigment R which absorbs longer wavelength light and is important for our perception of red. The brain interprets the colour of an object by comparing the intensity of the signals from the three types of cones.

SAQ 5.4

The structure of the molecules of pigment R and pigment G are extremely similar, and the genes that code for them lie next to each other on the X chromosome. It is not uncommon for these genes to become combined so that between them they code for only one type of pigment.

a Suggest how the vision of a person whose genes for pigments R and G had combined would be affected.

b Explain why this defect in vision is much more common in men than in women.

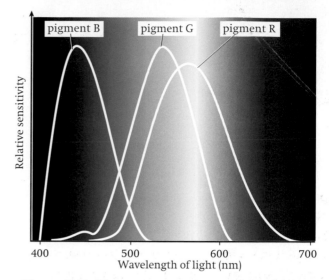

● **Figure 5.11** The response patterns of the three cone pigments to different wavelengths of light.

Release of neurotransmitter from rods and cones

Before we consider how rods and cones react to changes in the potential across their membranes, first think back to what you know about action potentials in neurones, and about synapses. You may remember that the presynaptic membrane of a neurone only releases transmitter substance when an action potential arrives (*Biology 2*, pages 110–14). The action potential is a fleeting **depolarisation** of the plasma membrane – that is, the normal resting potential of about −70 mV is momentarily reduced in magnitude. (Indeed, it very briefly swings right around in the other direction, so that the inside of the membrane is momentarily more *positive* than the outside).

Neither rod nor cone cells ever generate action potentials, no matter what the potential difference across their membranes. However, we have seen that they are most depolarised when they are *not* receiving light; that is, when their membrane potential has a magnitude of only −40 mV. Stimulation with light, far from depolarising them, does exactly the opposite – it *increases* the magnitude of the membrane potential to −70 mV, making them hyperpolarised.

So, surprising as it may at first seem, there is logic in the fact that rods and cones release transmitter substance into the synaptic cleft between themselves and bipolar cells when *no* light is falling on them, and they *stop* releasing transmitter substance when they are illuminated. Several different transmitter substances are released from rod cells. The one released from cone cells is always **glutamate**.

The roles of bipolar cells and ganglion cells

The transmitter released by a resting rod or cone diffuses across the synaptic cleft and reaches a bipolar cell. The arrival of the transmitter either depolarises or hyperpolarises the bipolar cell, which either increases or decreases the amount of transmitter substance that it releases. (Different bipolar cells react differently.) This transmitter diffuses across the synaptic cleft, and slots into receptors on the plasma membrane of a ganglion cell. Ganglion cells are never totally inactive, always firing off action potentials which travel along the optic nerve to the brain. However, the frequency with which these action potentials are produced varies according to the amount of transmitter arriving from the bipolar cells. Some ganglion cells fire more slowly when the rods or cones that are feeding information to them are illuminated and stop releasing transmitter substance, while others fire more frequently.

Visual acuity

The different patterns of connections between rods and cones and bipolar cells are responsible for differences in sharpness, or **resolution**, of the images that we see when light falls onto different parts of the eye. The resolution of the image that is perceived by the brain is sometimes known as **visual acuity**.

Many rod cells form synapses with the same bipolar cell. So information from many rod cells is

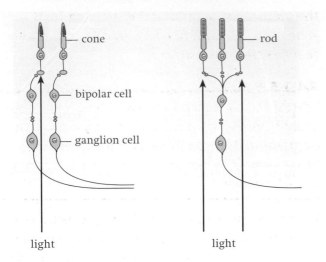

- **Figure 5.12** Visual acuity using rods and cones. Information from rods is pooled, so they are not as good as cones in providing detailed images.

combined together. This helps with the detection of dim light, because the small responses of many rod cells can be pooled to produce a larger response that can be detected in the brain. However, this pooling of information means that the brain is not aware of the individual responses of individual rod cells, only an averaging of the response from a collection of them. In effect, it is as though the perceived image is made up of a few large dots rather than many small ones – the resolution, or visual acuity, is poor (*figure 5.12*).

This is not true for cone cells, where each bipolar cell receives inputs from only a very few cones. Indeed, in the middle of the fovea, each bipolar cell only receives inputs from a single cone cell.

The brain therefore receives information from each cone cell separately, and this produces a high-resolution perceived image. This is also helped by the fact that cones are concentrated in the fovea, where the image that forms on the retina is sharpest and least distorted. Rods are concentrated in other regions of the retina, away from the fovea. The features of rods and cones are summarised in *table 5.2*.

The brain and perception of images

The images that we see in our minds are not just simple copies of the image that falls onto the retina of the eye. The brain takes information from the retina and processes it to form the perceived image.

Indeed, even before the information reaches the brain, quite a lot of processing has already taken place in the retina itself. The different patterns of connections between the receptor cells (rods and cones), bipolar cells and ganglion cells mean that the nerve impulses that are eventually fired off to the brain carry information not only about the shapes and colours of the objects we are looking at, but also other features such as the relative brightness of each object compared to the others, and their movement.

As they pass into the brain, the nerve impulses travel along three different pathways. One pathway carries patterns of nerve impulses that convey information about colour, another about

Rods	Cones
Very high sensitivity – can respond to just a single photon of light; specialised for night vision	Lower sensitivity – specialised for day vision
Contain more photopigment than cones, so can capture more light	Contain less photopigment than rods
Respond relatively slowly to light, so not sensitive to rates of 'flicker' above about 12 Hz	Respond more quickly to light, so are sensitive to rates of 'flicker' up to 55 Hz
Only one type of pigment, so do not distinguish between different wavelengths (colours) of light vision	Three different types of cone cell, each with a different type of pigment sensitive to a different range of wavelengths, so provide colour vision
Information from many rod cells converges on a single ganglion cell, so give low visual acuity	Information from each cone cell goes to only one or two ganglion cells, so give high visual acuity
Not present in the centre of the fovea	Mostly found in the fovea, especially tightly packed in the centre of it

- **Table 5.2** Features of rods and cones.

shapes, and the third about movement and spatial relationships. Each pathway is made up of millions of neurones. Moreover, there are interconnections between the three pathways, so a highly sophisticated type of **parallel processing** is going on in the brain. And, at the same time, other information is flowing into these pathways from other parts of the brain, for example from areas concerned with memory or with hearing. The 'picture' that we see in our mind is the result of integration of information in these three pathways, so that what we 'see' is much, much more than a straightforward photograph of the world around us. (For comparison, a desktop computer uses only sequential processing, not the much more sophisticated parallel processing. Visual analysis by the brain uses more computing power than even a supercomputer can cope with.)

An analysis of optical illusions can begin to give us a little insight into the way in which processing in the brain affects our perceived image. For example, in *figure 5.13a*, most people can easily see both rows and columns of dots. In *b*, however, you will almost certainly see columns in the top diagram and rows in the bottom one –

the brain is using information arriving from your retina about differences in colour to ensure that you 'see' this pattern.

SAQ 5.5

What is the difference in the visual image that your brain is producing when you look at the two diagrams in *figure 5.13c*? What is the difference between the information that the brain is receiving from the two images?

In general, the way that the brain processes the nerve impulses arriving from the retina appears to have evolved so that the image we see provides us with what is likely to be the most useful information about our environment. So, for example, if we see one person standing close to us and another person some distance away, we do not 'see' the first person as big and the second as small – even though this is what the image on the retina is recording. The brain takes the information from the retina, and other information from other parts of the brain, to put the most likely interpretation on what the retinal image actually means, in this case that both people are about the same size, and that one person is further away than the other. In some cases, the brain will even create information that is not there at all, building patterns that 'ought' to be there but in reality are not.

SAQ 5.6

What part of the images that you can see in *figure 5.14* is purely a result of creative 'filling-in' by the brain?

● **Figure 5.13** An optical illusion.

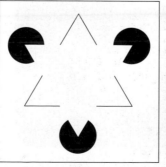 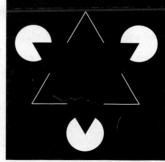

● **Figure 5.14** Another optical illusion – the Kaniza triangle.

The effects of ageing on vision

As we age, our vision tends to become less acute. There is more than one reason for this. For example, we have seen that most people lose a considerable degree of elasticity in the lenses of the eyes as they age. So, when the ciliary muscles contract to focus onto a near object, loosening the tension of the suspensory ligaments, the lens no longer springs back into a fat, rounded shape. It remains relatively thin, so that the light rays are not bent as much as they should be, and the image of the object is not focused clearly on the retina. Similarly, the lens is less able to be stretched out when focusing on distant objects. Many older people find that, even if their vision was perfect in their youth, they now need to wear glasses both for close focusing and for looking into the distance.

Cataracts

Another problem that frequently develops as a person ages is that the lens becomes less transparent. The lens is made of living cells, and as a person ages the proteins that they contain may begin to denature. If the proteins coagulate, then part of the lens becomes cloudy white, a condition known as **cataract** (*figure 5.15*).

Some degree of opacity of the lens develops in many people as they age, but in most cases the condition does not affect vision badly enough to require treatment. When it does, the lens is usually completely removed. The operation is a simple one, and can be done under local

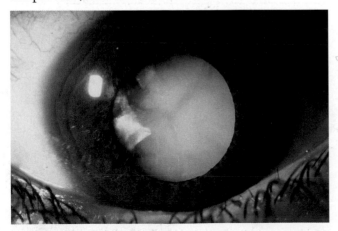

● **Figure 5.15** An eye showing a cataract. The cloudy appearance is due to denaturing of proteins in the lens.

anaesthetic. The person then needs to wear glasses to make up for the loss of the ability of the eye to bend light rays by as much as it could before. Alternatively, an artificial lens may be implanted into the eye to take the place of the living one.

SAQ 5.7

Explain why a person whose lens has been removed, or replaced with an artificial lens, will still need two pairs of glasses – one for near vision and one for distant vision.

The ear

The ear is responsible for the senses of hearing, balance and the detection of movement of the head. Like the eye and any other sense organ, it contains receptor cells which respond to environmental changes by generating nerve impulses that are sent to the brain for processing.

The structure of the ear

Figure 5.16 shows the structure of the human ear. It can be considered as having three main parts – the outer, middle and inner ear.

The **outer ear** comprises the **pinna**, **auditory canal** and **tympanic membrane** (ear drum). The pinna probably does not have an important role in humans, but in many animals it helps to collect sound waves and direct them towards the tympanic membrane. (In some animals that live in hot climates, such as elephants and fennec foxes, the pinna has a secondary role of providing a large surface area through which heat can be lost.) Sound waves travel as a series of rarefactions and compressions in the air inside the auditory canal, and this in turn results in vibrations of the tympanic membrane.

The **middle ear**, like the outer ear, contains air. Within it are three small bones, the **auditory ossicles**, which are arranged in such a way that the vibrations of the eardrum are amplified as they pass through them. The first of these ossicles, the **malleus** ('hammer') is attached to the centre of the tympanic membrane, and makes contact with the second ossicle, the **incus** ('anvil'). The third ossicle,

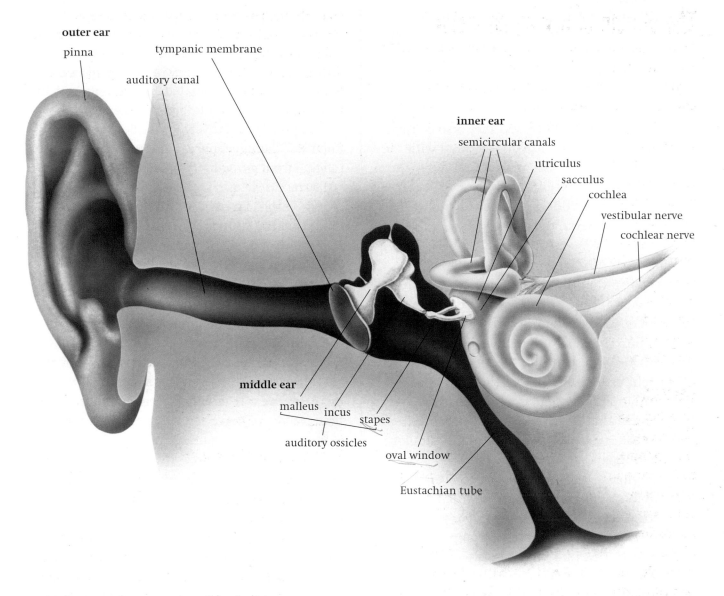

outer ear
pinna
tympanic membrane
auditory canal

inner ear
semicircular canals
utriculus
sacculus
cochlea
vestibular nerve
cochlear nerve

middle ear
malleus
incus
stapes
auditory ossicles
oval window
Eustachian tube

● **Figure 5.16** The structure of the human ear.

the **stapes** ('stirrup'), transmits the vibrations from the incus to the membrane of the **oval window**. The ossicles are held in position by ligaments. An air-filled passageway, the **Eustachian tube**, leads from the middle ear into the back of the throat. When you swallow, the entrance to this tube opens, so that there is direct contact between the air in your mouth and the air in the middle ear. This helps to ensure that the air pressure on both sides of the tympanic membrane stays approximately the same. If you have flown in an aircraft, in which air pressure is kept lower than normal, you may have felt the uncomfortable sensation that results from the air pressure inside your middle ear staying at one level, while the air pressure in your outer ear drops or rises as the aircraft changes altitude. Having a

cold may also cause discomfort, as the Eustachian tube can become partly blocked by mucus.

The **inner ear**, unlike the other two areas, contains fluid. It is embedded within the bones of the skull. The most striking part of it is the **cochlea**, and it is here that the receptor cells are found which convert the energy in sound waves into the energy in a nerve impulse. The receptor cells are arranged into a structure called the **organ of Corti**, which runs all along the **basilar membrane**, through the whole length of the coiled cochlea. When the oval window vibrates, these vibrations are transmitted through the fluid in the cochlea, and cause these receptor cells to vibrate as well. The cells have tiny, stiff hairs called **stereocilia** on their upper surface which are embedded in another membrane, and are known as **hair cells**. They are in close contact with the neurones that form the **cochlear nerve**.

As well as the cochlea, the inner ear also contains three **semicircular canals**, and two chambers called the **utriculus** and **sacculus**. These, too, are full of fluid, and they also contain hair cells. This part of the ear is involved with the sense of balance. Impulses from it pass along the **vestibular nerve**. This joins with the cochlear nerve, to form the **auditory nerve** which transmits impulses to the brain.

Hearing

We have seen that the structure of the ear allows vibrations in the air (sound waves) to be transmitted from outside the body, through the middle ear and into the fluid of the cochlea (*figure 5.17*). These vibrations cause vibration of the hair cells.

The hair cells maintain a resting potential across their plasma membranes in a similar way to neurones, that is their sodium–potassium pumps push sodium ions out and potassium ions in, resulting in a negative potential inside. When the cells vibrate, they are depolarised. This causes them to release neurotransmitter, which causes depolarisation of the endings of nerve cells in the cochlear nerve. This generates action potentials which are carried into the brain.

The brain can determine the **frequency** (pitch) of a sound by detecting which neurones are conducting the nerve impulses into it. The hair cells nearest to the oval window are receptive to high frequency (high-pitched) sounds, while those furthest from it are receptive to low frequency (low-pitched) sounds. The brain also uses differences in the frequency of the impulses to help with discrimination between low-pitched and very low-pitched sounds, because the deepest sounds produce relatively few, widely spaced impulses. Young people are able to hear sounds ranging from a frequency of about 20 Hz to 20 000 Hz. As we age, we lose the ability to hear sounds at the extremes of this range, especially higher-pitched sounds. This loss begins quite early in life, and even people in their early 20s may already have a smaller range of hearing than a teenager. By old age, most people can no longer hear sounds with frequencies above about 8000 Hz.

The **loudness** of a sound, too, is determined partly by the frequency of the action potentials arriving in the brain. Loud sounds cause a greater amplitude of vibration in the hair cells, and this increases the rate at which action potentials are fired off by the nerve cells in the cochlear nerve. Moreover, there are some hair cells which appear not to respond at all except when the sound is very loud. If impulses are generated from these cells, then this provides additional information that the sound is indeed extremely loud.

The **direction** of a sound is determined by the differences in the impulses coming from the two ears. The brain uses two types of information for this. It can compare the loudness and the **timing** of the sounds in each ear. The ear nearest to the source of the sound will detect a louder sound,

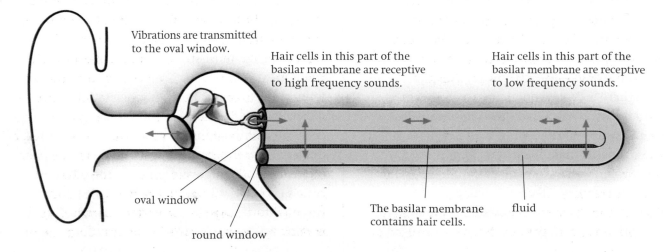

Vibrations are transmitted to the oval window.

Hair cells in this part of the basilar membrane are receptive to high frequency sounds.

Hair cells in this part of the basilar membrane are receptive to low frequency sounds.

oval window

round window

The basilar membrane contains hair cells.

fluid

● **Figure 5.17** The role of the cochlea in hearing.

and will detect it a fraction of a section before the other ear.

Balance

Our sense of balance depends on receptor cells in the semicircular canals, the utriculus and the sacculus. These receptor cells form synapses with sensory endings of the vestibular nerve. The nerve cells in the vestibular nerve are constantly firing action potentials off to the brain, and it is changes in the patterns of these impulses that the brain interprets to provide information about the position of the head, and the rate and direction of its movement.

In both the utriculus and the sacculus, there is a patch of cells called a **macula**. The maculae are each about 2 mm across, and are covered with a gelatinous layer containing many tiny crystals of calcium carbonate, called **otoliths**. Each macula contains numerous **hair cells** – receptor cells which, like those in the cochlea, have stiff stereocilia ('hairs') projecting from their upper surfaces. The ends of the cilia are embedded in the gelatinous layer, and they form synapses with neurones of the vestibular nerve.

These hair cells are sensitive to the orientation of the head. The otoliths are relatively heavy, and are pulled downwards by gravity. In any particular position of the head, the otoliths will pull the hairs of the hair cells in a particular direction. This causes sodium channels to open in some of the hair cells, depolarising them, and this then causes changes in the pattern of action potentials transmitted along the vestibular nerve. The maculae in the utriculus and the sacculus are orientated in different directions, so between them they provide complete information in three dimensions about exactly how the head is positioned. The hair cells in the utriculus lie mostly in the horizontal plane, and these sense orientation of the head when you are upright. The ones in the sacculus lie mostly in the vertical plane, and these sense orientation of the head when you are lying down.

Each of the three semicircular canals is filled with a viscous fluid. They each have a swelling at

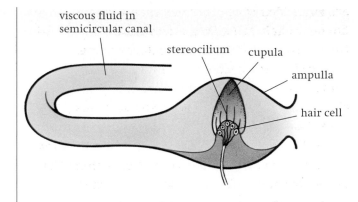

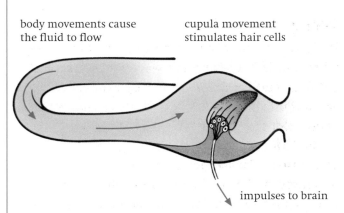

● **Figure 5.18** The role of the semicircular canals in sensing movement of the head.

one end called an **ampulla**. Inside each ampulla is a number of hair cells which have the ends of their cilia embedded in a gelatinous structure called a **cupula** (*figure 5.18*). The cupulas, unlike the otoliths, do not contain calcium carbonate. When the head moves, the inertia of the fluid in the semicircular canals causes it to get momentarily 'left behind', and it collects in the ampulla, exerting a force on the cupula and bending it to one side. The three ampullae are orientated in different directions, so that no matter what direction the head moves in, at least two of them will detect this movement. The movement of the cupula pulls on the cilia, causing depolarisation of the hair cells, and therefore a change in the pattern of impulses carried by the nerve cells in the vestibular nerve.

SUMMARY

◆ Sense organs contain receptor cells, which transfer energy in a stimulus into changes in electrical potential across the plasma membranes of neurones.

◆ The part of the eye that contains receptor cells is the retina. The cornea, aqueous humour, lens and vitreous humour refract light rays to bring them to a focus on the fovea of the retina.

◆ Light rays from nearby objects are diverging as they reach the eye, and need to be refracted strongly to bring them to a focus. This is achieved by contraction of the ciliary muscles which releases tension on the suspensory ligaments and allows the lens to form its natural, highly convex shape.

◆ Light rays from distant objects do not need to be refracted so strongly. Relaxation of the ciliary muscles increases tension on the suspensory ligaments, pulling the lens out into a thinner, less convex shape.

◆ The retina contains two types of receptor cells, rods and cones. Both have stacks of membranes in their outer segment in which are embedded pigment molecules. The sodium–potassium pump maintains a resting potential in rods and cones of about −40 mV inside.

◆ In rods, the pigment is rhodopsin. A rhodopsin molecule is made up of a protein, opsin, and a light-absorbing molecule called retinal. When light hits retinal, it changes shape, and this brings about changes in the permeability of the rod cell membrane to potassium and sodium ions, causing hyperpolarisation. Similar events occur when light strikes the pigments in a cone cell.

◆ Rod and cone cells continually release transmitter substance when they are not hit by light. When light strikes them, the resulting hyperpolarisation causes them to release less transmitter. This affects the polarisation of the bipolar cells with which they form synapses, and this in turn affects the frequency with which ganglion cells transmit action potentials along the optic nerve to the brain.

◆ There are three types of cone cells, each containing a different type of pigment sensitive to a different range of wavelengths of light. Cones are therefore responsible for colour vision.

◆ Signals from several different rod cells converge on one ganglion cell, so the brain does not receive information from individual rods and so does not 'see' a high-resolution image. The information from each cone cell in the centre of the fovea, however, is carried individually to one ganglion cell, so cones provide a higher-resolution image than rods.

◆ Perception of images is a result not only of the image that forms on the retina, but also of the processing of this image in the retina and in the brain.

◆ The lens may develop cloudy areas as it ages, a condition known as a cataract. If the symptoms are great enough to require treatment, the lens can be removed in a simple surgical operation.

◆ The cochlea in the ear is responsible for hearing. Vibrations caused by sound waves are transmitted to hair cells, which depolarise as they are vibrated. This sets up action potentials which are carried to the brain.

◆ The semicircular canals, utriculus and sacculus are responsible for balance. Changes in orientation of the head, or in rate or direction of movement, cause depolarisation of hair cells which results in changes in the pattern of action potentials transmitted to the brain.

Questions

1 a Explain what is meant by *accommodation* in the eye, and describe how it is brought about.
   b Explain why accommodation cannot be achieved in the eye of a person who has been treated for a cataract.

2 a Describe the structure of the retina.
   b Explain how the organisation of the cells in the retina can explain the fact that the acuity of vision in dim light is much less than that in bright light.

3 Compare and contrast the structures and functions of rod cells and cone cells.

4 Describe how the structure of the ear is related to its function in:
   a hearing;
   b balance.

6

Behaviour

By the end of this chapter you should be able to:

1 explain, with reference to their biological significance, what is meant by innate behaviour, instinct and reflex action;

2 describe one example of a reflex action;

3 explain that some behaviour can be interpreted in terms of stereotyped, automatic responses, and that these can be modified by environmental stimuli;

4 outline the methods and conclusions of the classic experiments to investigate the nature of learned behaviour, with reference to the work of Pavlov on conditioning, the work of Skinner on operant conditioning and the work of Kohler on intelligent behaviour in chimpanzees.

The study of animal behaviour is concerned with everything that an animal does – sleeping, being aggressive, standing still, making sounds and so on. Although people have been interested in animal behaviour for thousands of years, its beginnings as an area of scientific investigation can probably be said to have occurred in the early years of the twentieth century.

These early studies grew partly out of Darwin's ideas on evolution by natural selection, so that some people began to look for the ways in which particular patterns of behaviour might adapt living organisms to their environments. This type of study became known as **ethology**. Ethologists tended to study the natural behaviour of animals in their natural environments. They were interested in the evolutionary basis of behaviour, and they tended to focus on simple, inherited behaviour patterns.

At the same time, other investigators were taking a very different approach. They carried out their experiments in laboratories, under controlled conditions, and they were especially interested in how animals learned new patterns of behaviour. This type of study became known as **psychology**, and often focused on differences between the behaviour patterns of different animal species, when it was known as comparative psychology. Some psychologists concentrated on studying behavioural events involving stimuli and responses, and how rewards and punishments could affect these responses; these studies were known as **behaviouralism**.

Throughout the first half of the twentieth century, these two different approaches towards studying animal behaviour – those of ethologists and of psychologists/behaviouralists – gave rise to the so-called 'nature/nurture' debate – is an animal's behaviour largely controlled by its 'nature', that is its genes, or by its 'nurture', that is the experiences that it has during its lifetime?

Today, there is no sharp divide between these two approaches to studying and interpreting animal behaviour and, as we shall see, there is now an understanding that 'nature' and 'nurture' both contribute to most behaviour patterns. Other ways of studying animal behaviour have also emerged, in particular the physiological approach, in which the roles of receptors, neurones and effectors in bringing about behaviour are investigated.

So, animal behaviour is now a very diverse and extensive branch of science. This chapter will give you just a very small taste of this diversity. We will look at two aspects of it – firstly the importance of instinctive behaviour patterns, and secondly some classic early experiments into the ways in which animals learn. And, although we are especially interested here in the behaviour of mammals, we will also look at examples from other groups in the animal kingdom, because their relatively simple behaviour compared with that of some mammals has made them good subjects for research.

Innate behaviour

As we watch the behaviour of animals, we often find ourselves amazed at the way in which they seem to 'know' how to behave. For example, a dragonfly nymph crawls out of the pond in which it has spent the first few years of its life, and drags itself up a plant stem until it is well above the water surface. It attaches its feet very firmly, and hangs on as its skin splits. As its body emerges from the old skin, it at first hangs downwards, until a moment arrives when it suddenly twists upwards and grabs onto the stem with its newly-emerged legs. It stays in this position for quite a long time, as its new wings gradually expand and dry. After some time – sometimes several hours – it quickly cleans its large eyes with its front pair of legs then takes off on its very first flight (*figure 6.1*).

How does the dragonfly nymph 'know' how to do all of these things? Until the moment that it crawls up onto the plant stem, it has spent its whole life under water. Until the moment that it first takes off, it has never used wings. Yet these actions are carried out with perfection, the very first time that they are used.

This behaviour is an example of **innate** or **instinctive** behaviour. (The two words are used interchangeably.) Innate behaviour can be defined as a *pattern of inherited, pre-set behaviour that does not require learning or practice*. We must assume that the dragonfly nymph does not 'know' what to do in the sense that it thinks about it and makes decisions. The pattern of behaviour that it shows is simply a result of the 'wiring' of its nervous system, and it is inherited in just the same way as, for example, the growth of its wings, the colour of its body or the structure of its excretory system.

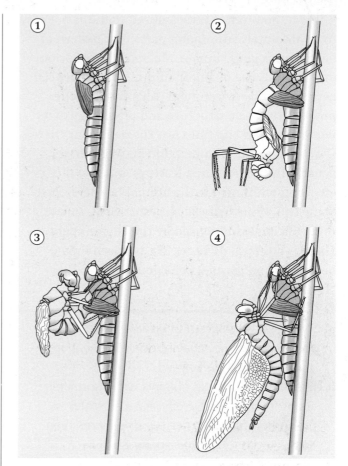

● **Figure 6.1** A dragonfly nymph follows an innate, complex pattern of behaviour as it changes into an adult.

Genes and behaviour

At the beginning of the twentieth century, many ethologists considered that much of the behaviour that they observed, especially in animals other than mammals, was entirely innate. Such behaviour patterns are often stereotyped, that is they are always performed in the same way by all the members of a particular species. Innate behaviour patterns can be assumed to be 'hard-wired' into the animal's brain; it has inherited genes that somehow programme its nervous system to carry out this behaviour. The evolution of this kind of behaviour can be thought of in just the same way as the evolution of any other characteristic. Animals that have alleles that produce behaviour patterns that give them a selective advantage are more likely to survive and breed than animals whose alleles produce less well-adapted behaviour patterns. So, over time, the alleles that produce the best type of behaviour become more and more common in a population.

Today, however, it is recognised that it is not easy to be absolutely sure that a particular pattern of behaviour is *purely* innate. Much of the behaviour of animals is the result of an interaction between genes and the environment. An animal's genes produce the basic structure and physiology of its nervous system and muscles. The behaviour that it shows is a result of interaction between these genetically-programmed features and also the environment in which the animal has developed. Some behaviours may be almost entirely innate, others strongly influenced by the environment. There is no sharp dividing line between innate behaviour and learned behaviour.

SAQ 6.1

a Suggest advantages and disadvantages to an animal of having behaviour patterns that are innate, rather than learned.

b It is often found that animals with short life-spans (such as a housefly) have a greater proportion of innate behaviour patterns than animals with longer life-spans (such as elephants). Suggest why this may be so.

SAQ 6.2

Genes are not the only way in which behaviour patterns can be passed on from generation to generation. How else may this occur?

Reflexes

A reflex action can be defined as a relatively rapid, automatic response to a stimulus. In respect of human behaviour, we could perhaps also add that reflex actions do not involve conscious thought, but this is a dangerous statement to make if we are describing the behaviour of other animals, as it is impossible to tell whether or not conscious thought is going on in an animal's brain.

In a simple reflex action, action potentials pass along a pathway of neurones known as a **reflex arc**. A receptor picks up information (the stimulus) from the environment, and action potentials pass along a sensory neurone to the brain or the spinal cord (see also chapter 4). They then pass into an intermediate neurone and from

there to a motor neurone. This carries action potentials to an effector which brings about a response. All of this happens automatically. The pathway along which the action potentials travel after a particular receptor has received a particular stimulus is always the same, so the response that it elicits is always the same.

Reflexes may be very rapid and brief behaviour patterns. For example, a sudden bang will make you blink (the 'startle reflex'). A sharp tap on the knee will make your lower leg lift upwards. The iris reflex, described on page 54, is another example of a fast-acting, short-lived reflex action.

Other reflexes may involve rather longer-term behaviour. For example, when we stand in a particular position, muscles in the legs and other parts of the body are being held in a particular level of tension. But, however still we try to stand, slight variations are always occurring, and we are constantly making numerous small changes in muscle tension to stop ourselves from falling over (*figure 6.2*). A constant flurry of information from stretch receptors in the muscles passes to the central nervous system along sensory neurones,

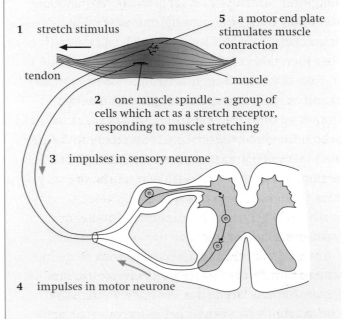

1   stretch stimulus

5   a motor end plate stimulates muscle contraction

tendon

muscle

2   one muscle spindle – a group of cells which act as a stretch receptor, responding to muscle stretching

3   impulses in sensory neurone

4   impulses in motor neurone

● **Figure 6.2** As a person stands still, stretch receptors in the posture muscles constantly send impulses to the central nervous system, resulting in impulses passing back to the muscle which responds by contracting or relaxing to maintain the body position. This is a reflex action.

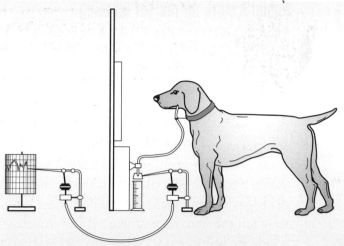

● **Figure 6.5** One of Pavlov's experiments into classical conditioning. A tube in the dog's cheek collects saliva, and the volume that is collected is recorded on the kymograph drum. Pavlov used this apparatus to investigate the response of the dog's salivary glands to different types and strengths of stimuli.

found that at first the dog just pricked up its ears when it heard the bell, but of course did not salivate. However, after several sessions when the ringing bell preceded the giving of food, the dog began to salivate when it heard the bell. The more times this was done, the more saliva the dog produced at the sound of the bell alone, and the more quickly the saliva was produced.

The dog had learned to associate the sound of the bell with the arrival of food. This kind of learning is called **classical conditioning**.

To begin with, the dog had a reflex action – the production of saliva in response to the taste or smell of food. As far as we know, this is an innate response; that is, the dog was just born with it and did not have to learn it. The stimulus of the taste or smell of food is known as the **unconditioned stimulus**. The new stimulus which the dog learned to associate with food – the sound of the bell – is known as the **conditioned stimulus**. The whole reflex, that is the response to the new stimulus, is a **conditioned reflex**.

Skinner's work on operant conditioning

Even though Pavlov's experiments were very well controlled, he found that his dogs were learning rather more than he had intended. For example, hungry dogs quickly realised that they were going to be fed when the experimenter came along to take them into the laboratory, and would run ahead, tail wagging, ready to be placed in their harness. This involves a more complex process than is being measured with the salivation reflex, because here the dog is making a decision about where and how to move. Such an activity, where an animal learns to carry out a behaviour that makes something good happen to it, is known as **operant conditioning**.

B. F. Skinner was not the first person to investigate operant conditioning, but he became very well known for his invention of the 'Skinner box' (*figure 6.6*). A Skinner box is a cage in which an animal can be placed, containing a bar that the animal can press, or a key that it can peck. A reward of some kind – often food – is provided when the animal carries out this action. At first, the animal simply moves around in the box looking for a way out. Eventually, often just by chance, it presses the bar and a reward appears. After this has happened once, twice or a few times, the animal begins purposefully to press the bar. It has learned to associate this behaviour with the reward.

● **Figure 6.6** B. F. Skinner with a Skinner box.

Similar results are seen if, rather than being presented with a reward, the animal is able to avoid something unpleasant by pressing the bar. For example, a rat in a Skinner box will quickly learn to press a bar to switch off a very bright light just above its head, or to stop a mild electric shock.

The adaptive value of conditioning

Both classical conditioning and operant conditioning can be described as **associative learning**. In each case, the animal learns to associate a stimulus or an action that previously had meant nothing to it with some rewarding results. It changes its behaviour in such a way that the rewarding results – often known as a **reinforcer** – are achieved more often.

At the beginning of this section, our definition of learning included a statement that it had adaptive value. It is not too difficult to see that associative learning does, indeed, increase the chances of an animal's survival and reproductive success. For example, imagine a young insect-eating bird that tries to eat a wasp. This is likely to be an unpleasant experience, and the bird quickly learns to associate yellow and black with something that is best not tasted. In the future, it will avoid not only yellow and black wasps, but also yellow and black caterpillars, yellow and black beetles, and anything else that is yellow and black.

● **Figure 6.7** Chimpanzees are able to learn quite complex tasks involving the use of tools. This one uses a stick to extract insects from holes in a log.

Kohler's work on insight learning

In 1927, Wolfgang Kohler wrote a book called *The Mentality of Apes*. This book described his work on the behaviour of chimpanzees. Some of the results of his experiments indicated that relatively 'intelligent' animals, such as primates, can learn in a more complex way than the types of associative learning described above (*figure 6.7*).

One of Kohler's chimps was known as Sultan. When a banana was placed on the ground outside his cage, Sultan quickly learned to use a long stick to reach the banana and work it into his cage where he would eat it. When he had learned to do this, Kohler gave him not one but two sticks that could be made to fit together end-to-end. Again a banana was placed outside the cage, but this time too far away to be reached with one stick.

Sultan tried to reach the banana with a stick, and failed. He then tried putting one stick down outside the cage, and pushing it forward with the second stick until it touched the banana. But, of course, he could not rake the banana back. After an hour or so, he eventually gave up, and moved off to a different part of the cage to play, taking the sticks with him.

While playing, Sultan suddenly realised that the end of one stick could be pushed into the end of the other stick. Straight away, he rushed back to the side of the cage and used his extended stick to rake in the banana. Other chimps showed similar abilities, for example stacking up boxes so that they could stand on them to take a banana hanging above their reach.

This type of learning seems to be something altogether more complex than the simple associative learning described by Pavlov and Skinner. It has been termed **insight learning**, because it seemed as though inspiration suddenly struck the chimps, often while they were doing something not directly connected with obtaining the food. Some form of reasoning seems to be going on in the animals' brains – they are working out how a particular pattern of behaviour might solve a problem.

Many investigators see insight learning in chimps as evidence that the chimps are *thinking* about the problem, in a similar way to the ways that we go about problem-solving. Perhaps the

Box 6A The physiological basis of memory

What exactly is going on in our brains when we remember things? This is not an easy question to answer in respect of the human brain, partly because of its tremendous complexity – far in excess of a super-computer – and partly because it is extremely difficult to carry out controlled investigations into physiological changes happening in a working human brain during the storing of memories and their recall. However, considerable work has been done on memory in organisms with less complex nervous systems, and also in several species of mammals other than humans.

The sea hare, *Aplysia*, is a large, dark-brown sea slug (*figure 6.8*) – a marine mollusc that is a close relative of the slugs and snails that are common in gardens. It can sometimes be seen in rock pools at low tide, browsing on seaweeds. It has a simple nervous system containing only about 20 000 neurones, each of which is much larger than those in mammals, and this makes it relatively easy to study the changes that take place in these cells as a sea hare learns.

Sea hares exchange gases through gills on their upper surface. When this surface is touched, the gills are withdrawn into the sea hare's body. However, if this happens repeatedly and no harm is done, the sea hare eventually learns not to withdraw the gills. This is an example of habituation, like that of the clamworms described on page 86. It is now known that this happens because of changes in what happens at the synapses in the neural pathway leading from the receptors that detect the touch, to the muscles that withdraw the gills. Normally, when an action potential arrives at a presynaptic neurone, calcium channels open and calcium ions flood in, causing vesicles of transmitter substance to fuse with the presynaptic membrane and release the transmitter into the synaptic cleft. But as more and more action potentials arrive at a synapse, there is less and less effect on the calcium channels, so the amount of calcium ions entering the neurone decreases. So less and less transmitter substance is released, until eventually there is not enough to produce an action potential in the postsynaptic neurone.

Another type of simple learning shown by sea hares is called **sensitisation**. Here, just before the dorsal surface is touched, the sea hare is given an unpleasant stimulus, such as an electric shock. It quickly learns to withdraw its gills even faster and further than usual. It can 'remember' this for several days. In this case, the synaptic connections are actually *strengthened*, by changes that take place in the membrane of the presynaptic neurone so that even more calcium ions than usual are allowed into the cell. Moreover, over longer periods of time, neurones in frequently-used neural pathways actually grow new synapses.

How do these findings relate to human memory? Certainly all of the events involved in learning in sea hares do take place in human nervous systems as we learn. But obviously learning in humans is a much more complex process than in sea hares. Whereas a sea hare has 20 000 neurones, we have around 200×10^{12} neurones in the brain alone.

The memory of humans (and many other animals, too) can be considered to be made up of different types. Events that have happened very recently are stored in **short-term memory**, and some of these are then transferred into **long-term memory**. Studies of people with damage to the base of the forebrain, especially in the area of the thalamus and hippocampus, show that they lose the ability to form new memories – they cannot remember things for more than a few seconds. However, their memory for events that happened before the brain damage occurred is normal. This suggests that these parts of the brain are involved in short-term memory and the formation of new long-term memories. We can imagine that formation of new memories will involve changes at synapses like those described in the sea hare, plus perhaps many others that we have not yet been able to identify. For example, it is known that the hippocampus of a rat produces several thousand new neurones each day, and recent research suggests that this is a very important process for the formation of new memories.

Although the hippocampus is known to be important in the formation of human memories, many other parts of the brain are also involved in long-term memory storage. One idea is that the hippocampus holds memories temporarily, before transferring them to other parts of the brain, such as the cerebral cortex. The way in which these long-term memories are stored is not known, though it certainly must involve changes at synapses and the formation of new synapses.

Our brains handle different kinds of memory in different ways. **Explicit** memories are things that we know we know – we think about them consciously when recalling them. For example, if you have learned the names and functions of all the parts of the human eye, you can recall this when asked about it in an examination. **Implicit** memories are memories that we are not aware of – for example, you had to learn to ride a bicycle but you now do it without thinking about it. There is evidence that the ways in which explicit and implicit memories are acquired and stored are different from each other, and involve different parts of the brain. Always, though, it is changes at synapses, or formation of new ones, that seem to be at the heart of the mechanism by which we learn and remember.

● **Figure 6.8** The sea hare, *Aplysia*.

chimps think through the possible things that they might do to reach the high bunch of bananas, and work out in their heads that *this* action might produce *that* result. From watching other forms of behaviour in chimps, most people would agree that this is probably true. We do not find it difficult to imagine that the processes going on inside a chimpanzee's brain might be similar to what we know happens inside our own brain.

However, it is not easy to be sure that insight learning really does provide evidence of rational thinking. A real difficulty with experiments into insight behaviour is that they cannot, by their very nature, be repeated. The description above of Sultan's use of the two sticks is really no more than an *anecdote* – a story describing something interesting happening, that does not have the rigour and repeatability that we would want to see from a scientific investigation. The chimp's behaviour could just have happened by chance.

Other experiments suggest that similar learning can occur in several species of birds, including pigeons. For example, some pigeons were trained to push a box towards a green spot on the floor, but not to push the box if there was no green spot. This was done by rewarding them for the action when there was a green spot, but not when there wasn't a green spot. They were also trained to stand on a box placed underneath a banana hanging above them, so that they could peck at it. When they were put into a cage with a box, but no green spot, and a banana hanging above them, they first of all tried to reach the banana by standing on the floor underneath it. Then, quite suddenly, as though they had just seen the solution, they pushed the box underneath the banana and stood on it. This behaviour is not really all that different from that of the chimp described above. So, do pigeons show insight learning? Do birds think rationally? Only pigeons that had been taught both to push a box and to stand on one to reach a banana were able to come up with the solution of pushing the box underneath the banana – pigeons that had been taught just one of these actions never did manage to solve the problem. So the pigeons' prior learning was certainly very important in bringing about this new response. But whether or not any conscious, rational thought was going on in their brains is a question to which we still have no answers.

SUMMARY

◆ Innate or instinctive behaviour is a pattern of inherited, pre-set behaviour that does not require learning or practice.

◆ Most patterns of behaviour shown by animals are the result of genetically-determined features of the nervous system interacting with the environment in which the animal has developed.

◆ Innate, stereotyped patterns of behaviour can be modified by experience.

◆ A reflex action is one in which a particular stimulus brings about an automatic response. Some reflexes may be innate, for example the startle reflex when we respond to a sudden loud noise by blinking. Other reflexes may be learned, and are then known as conditioned reflexes.

◆ Pavlov showed that the salivation reflex of dogs in response to the sight of food could be modified so that it was also shown as a response to other stimuli, such as the sound of a bell. This is called classical conditioning.

◆ Skinner carried out experiments in which animals learned to carry out a particular action in order to obtain a reward or to avoid something unpleasant. This is known as operant conditioning.

◆ Kohler's work on chimpanzees showed that they were able to put together actions they had learned in two or more different situations to solve a particular problem. This is known as insight learning.

Questions

1 a Explain, with reference to examples, what is meant by *innate behaviour*.
   b What is the value of innate behaviour to living organisms?
   c Describe one example of the modification of an innate behaviour pattern in response to environmental stimuli.

2 Outline how the work of the following people has contributed to our knowledge of how animals learn:
   a Pavlov;
   b Skinner;
   c Kohler.

Answers to self-assessment questions

Chapter 1

1.1 Pepsin is a protease, and would break down proteins in the plasma membranes and cytoplasm of cells with which it came into contact. It is not activated until it has left the cells and is in the lumen of the stomach.

1.2 Secretin is secreted when acidic substances are present in the duodenum, and stimulates secretion of pancreatic juice containing HCO_3^- ions. These neutralise the hydrochloric acid from the stomach, providing a pH in which the pancreatic enzymes can work efficiently.

CCK is secreted when the products of fat and protein digestion are present in the duodenum. These substances will need further digestion before they can be absorbed. CCK stimulates the pancreas to secrete juices rich in enzymes, which catalyse these processes.

Thus the content of the pancreatic juice can be varied according to requirements, ensuring that, for example, enzymes are not wasted by being secreted unnecessarily.

1.3 Incisors: a human has two on each side of top jaw, two on each side of bottom jaw. A dog has three on each side of top jaw, three on each side of bottom jaw.

Canines: both dog and human have one on each side of top jaw, one on each side of bottom jaw.

Premolars and molars (it is not possible to tell them apart by looking at them in this way): a human has five on each side of top and bottom jaw. A dog has seven, four premolars and three molars on each side of top and bottom jaw.

1.4 Predators kill prey only rarely, and when they do there is likely to be great competition for the available food. It is therefore important for a predator to get as much of the prey inside its digestive system as quickly as possible, before other animals eat it.

1.5 Starch is a polymer of alpha-glucose molecules linked by glycosidic bonds between carbon atoms 1 and 4. Cellulose is a polymer of beta-glucose molecules, also linked by glycosidic bonds between carbon atoms 1 and 4. These different linkages mean that the shape of starch molecules is very different from the shape of cellulose molecules. Enzymes are specific to particular substrates, which must fit into and interact with their active sites. Different enzymes are therefore needed to catalyse the breakdown of starch and of cellulose.

Chapter 2

2.1 The blood in the hepatic portal vein will contain more carbon dioxide. If a meal has recently been eaten, then it may contain more monosaccharides, amino acids, vitamins, minerals and lipids (transported as lipoproteins) than the blood in the hepatic artery.

2.2 A condensation reaction; glycosidic bonds will be formed between glucose molecules.

2.3 They are insoluble in water, and so will not affect the water potential of the cell in which they are stored. They contain more energy per gram than either carbohydrates or proteins.

2.4 a They do not have mitochondria, in which all the stages of respiration except glycolysis take place. (Red blood cells rely on glycolysis to supply their ATP.)

b As they have no mitochondria, they cannot carry out Krebs cycle, only glycolysis.

2.5 a The ammonia will quickly dissolve in the large volumes of water around them, and be so diluted that it will not harm the fish.

b Turning ammonia into urea requires energy in the form of ATP, so by excreting ammonia rather than urea, significant amounts of energy are saved.

Chapter 3

3.1 Ventilation movements produced by contraction and relaxation of the intercostal muscles move the rib cage upwards for inspiration, and allow it to drop downwards during expiration. The cartilage at the ends of the ribs allows flexibility where they join to the sternum.

3.2 Finger joints and toe joints are hinge joints.

3.3 **a** Turning effect = force × distance from pivot
$$= 10\,N \times 0.3 \text{ metres}$$
$$= 3\,Nm$$
(Nm stands for newton metres)
b The turning effect exerted by the biceps muscle must equal the turning effect produced by the weight held in the hand.
So $3\,Nm = F \times 0.05\,m$
So $\quad F = 3 \div 0.05$
$$= 60\,N$$

3.4 **a** The TS shows the presence of both actin and myosin filaments and is therefore an A band.
b A TS across the H band would show only thick filaments. A TS across the I band would show only thin filaments.

3.5 ATP is needed for the myosin heads to detach from actin molecules. When ATP runs out, the myosin heads remain attached to the actin, so that the filaments cannot slide. The muscles are therefore locked in one position.

Chapter 4

4.1 A neurone is a single nerve cell. A nerve is a much larger structure, made up of the axons and dendrons of many neurones.

4.2 Faster heart-beat transfers oxygen to the muscles more rapidly, so that they can respire and produce ATP to enable them to contract; this is helpful for either tackling or running away from danger. Dilation of bronchi allows more air to enter and leave the lungs at each breath, which ensures that more oxygen can enter the blood more rapidly, and be transferred to the muscles. Dilation of pupils allows more light into the eye, which may help with receiving visual information about the danger. Sweating helps to remove some of the extra heat generated by the extra respiration happening in muscles. Erection of hairs can, in animals other than humans, make them look larger and so possibly discourage another animal from attacking them.

4.3 The sight, smell, taste or thought of food.

4.4 Blood pressure is likely to fall slightly.

4.5 The cerebellum is involved with the coordination of movements. Birds and fish fly and swim, so their movement often takes place in three dimensions. Most reptiles, however, mostly move along the ground, although some do swim or climb trees. On the whole, therefore, the coordination of the three-dimensional movements of birds and fish is likely to be more complex than the frequently two-dimensional movements of reptiles.

Chapter 5

5.1 Light has to pass through each of these structures before it reaches the retina. Blood would absorb and distort much of this light.

5.2 When looking at a close object, the person will normally be looking down, through the lower part of the lens. In order to see this object clearly, the light rays from it need to be bent inwards, and the converging lens helps with this.

When looking at a distant object, the person will normally be looking straight ahead, through the upper part of the lens. In order to see a distant object clearly, the degree to which the rays are bent needs to be decreased – hence the use of a diverging lens.

5.3 The radial muscles of the iris contract, so enlarging the diameter of the pupil and allowing more light to enter the eye.

5.4 **a** The person will not be able to distinguish between red and green.
b Men have one X and one Y chromosome, while women have two X chromosomes. The genes for the red and green pigments are on the X chromosome, but not on the Y. So men have only one copy of the genes for red and green pigments, while women have two. The allele that results in the abnormality of the pigments is recessive, so even if women have one copy of this allele, they still have normal pigments if the other allele is normal. Red–green colour-blindness is an example of a sex-linked condition.

5.5 You will see rows of dots in the top diagram, and columns of dots in the bottom one. Your brain is picking up tiny differences in the spacing between the dots – it is hard to see even when you are looking for it!

5.6 You can probably imagine a central triangle. There is no triangle there – the brain has filled this in from other elements of the pattern.

5.7 The function of the lens is to change shape to allow focusing on objects at different distances from the eye. If there is no lens present, or an artificial one that cannot change its shape, then this is not possible. Glasses are therefore needed to provide the different degree of refraction needed to focus on distant and near objects.

Chapter 6

6.1 **a** Innate behaviour patterns can be used immediately, and this may give considerable advantage to a young animal in, for example, a dangerous situation that it has not previously encountered. However, an innate response may not always be the best response to a particular stimulus. Learned behaviour patterns can help an animal to adapt to an environment during its life-time.

b Learning takes time. For a short-lived animal, there may simply not be enough time in its life-span for it to learn very much. For a long-lived animal, there is plenty of opportunity for learning.

6.2 Learning can take place as a young animal watches the behaviour of other members of its family or social group, and copies it. This is sometimes known as cultural learning.

6.3 **a** In many situations, a few milliseconds difference in the speed of a response can mean the difference between life and death.

b Reflex actions are most likely to be useful in fast-moving, threatening situations, such as attack by a predator.

6.4 The clamworm avoids wasting energy and losing valuable feeding time by withdrawing into the tube.

Glossary

absorption taking digested food substances from the lumen of the alimentary canal into cells and blood plasma.

accommodation altering the shape, and therefore the focal length, of the lens in order to focus on objects at different distances from the eye.

actin a protein that makes up the thin filaments in muscle.

adipose tissue a fat-storage tissue, in which each cell is almost filled with a large droplet of lipid.

alcohol dehydrogenase an enzyme found in the liver that catalyses the breakdown of ethanol to ethanal.

aldehyde dehydrogenase an enzyme found in the liver that catalyses the conversion of ethanal to ethanoate.

Alzheimer's disease a type of dementia, most commonly found in people over the age of 65, characterised by the formation of plaques of beta amyloid in the cerebral cortex.

ampulla a swelling at one end of a semicircular canal in the inner ear, containing receptor cells.

amylase an enzyme that catalyses the hydrolysis of starch to maltose.

antagonistic muscles a pair of muscles where the contraction of one pulls in the opposite direction to the contraction of the other.

aqueous humour a liquid that fills the part of the eye in front of the lens.

association area a part of the cerebrum in which information from various receptors is integrated.

autonomic ganglia a series of ganglia lying alongside the vertebral column, containing the cell bodies of neurones of the autonomic nervous system.

autonomic nervous system the motor neurones serving smooth muscle and internal organs.

autotroph an organism which can use an inorganic carbon source, such as carbon dioxide, and convert this to organic compounds using energy from sunlight or chemicals.

bile a greenish liquid containing bile salts, bile pigments and cholesterol, produced in the liver and stored in the gall bladder before being released into the duodenum.

bile salts sodium glycocholate and sodium taurocholate, present in bile; they help to emulsify fats in the duodenum.

bipolar cell one of the cells in the retina that collects information from the rods and cones, in the form of changes in membrane potential, and conveys it to the ganglion cells.

blind spot see optic disc.

brush border a surface of a cell which contains microvilli, so called because of its appearance under a microscope.

canaliculus a space between rows of hepatocytes in the liver, along which bile flows as it passes to the gall bladder and bile duct *or* a space containing a cytoplasmic process of an osteocyte in bone.

carboxypeptidase an enzyme produced by the epithelial cells of the villi in the small intestine, that breaks peptides into individual amino acids; it is an exopeptidase.

cataract a condition in which the lens becomes cloudy.

CCK a hormone secreted by the wall of the duodenum that stimulates the secretion of enzyme-rich pancreatic juice.

cerebellum the part of the brain that lies behind the cerebrum, which controls coordination of movement and posture.

cerebral cortex the outer, deeply-folded layer of the cerebrum, in which most high-order brain functions take place.

cerebral hemispheres the two hemispheres, right and left, that make up the cerebrum.

cerebrospinal fluid the fluid that surrounds the central nervous system, and fills the cavities within it.

chemical digestion the breakdown of large molecules into smaller ones by hydrolysis reactions, catalysed by enzymes.

chief cells cells in the wall of the stomach that secrete pepsinogen.

chondrocyte a cell found in cartilage.

choroid layer the tissue that lies between the retina and the sclera of the eye; its inner layer of cells contains melanin and so appears black.

chylomicron a type of lipoprotein.

chyme the mixture of partly-digested food, hydrochloric acid and enzymes that passes from the stomach into the duodenum.

chymotrypsin an enzyme produced in the pancreas that breaks down protein molecules into shorter chains of amino acids; it is an endopeptidase.

ciliary muscles a set of circular muscles in the ciliary body of the eye, whose contraction and relaxation alters the shape of the lens.

classical conditioning a type of learning in which an animal learns to respond to a stimulus which is different from the one that normally elicits the response.

cochlea the coiled, fluid-filled tube in the inner ear that contains receptor cells sensitive to sound.

conditioned reflex a reflex in which an animal has learned to respond to a different stimulus from the one that normally elicits the response.

cone a receptor cell in the retina of the eye; there are three types each receptive to a different range of wavelengths of light, so providing colour vision.

conjunctiva a thin layer of tissue that covers and protects the front of the eye.

cornea a thick, curved, transparent tissue at the front of the eye, that is responsible for most of the refraction of light as it enters the eye.

crypts of Lieberkühn the spaces between the villi in the ileum, where new cells are constantly being produced to replace old and damaged epithelial cells.

dark adaptation the adjustment of the eye to relatively dark conditions, which happens as opsin and retinal are converted to rhodopsin.

deamination the removal of the amine group from excess amino acids; the amine group is converted to urea for excretion, and the rest of the molecule respired or stored.

dementia a disease in which there is a general reduction of mental ability.

diastema a gap between the incisors and premolars in a herbivore, that allows manipulation of food in the mouth.

egestion the removal of undigested food as faeces from the anus.

emulsification the dispersal of tiny droplets of a water insoluble substance, such as fats, into water.

endopeptidase an enzyme that catalyses the hydrolysis of peptide bonds within a protein molecule.

enterokinase an enzyme that converts trypsinogen into trypsin in the duodenum.

Eustachian tube an air-filled passage that connects the middle ear to the throat.

exopeptidase an enzyme that breaks peptides into individual amino acids.

extensor a muscle whose contraction causes straightening at a joint.

fibril one of many structures found inside a muscle fibre.

flexor a muscle whose contraction causes bending at a joint.

fovea the part of the retina onto which light is focused when looking directly at an object; it contains densely-packed cones and is not covered by ganglion and bipolar cells.

ganglion cell one of the cells in the retina that receives information from bipolar cells; action potentials in the ganglion cells are carried along the optic nerve to the brain.

gastrin a hormone secreted by the wall of the stomach that stimulates the production of gastric juice.

glial cell a cell that, with neurones, makes up nervous tissue; Schwann cells are a type of glial cell.

globulin a type of plasma protein.

gluconeogenesis the production of glucose from other substances such as amino acids or fats.

glycogenolysis the breakdown of glycogen to glucose.

habituation a type of very simple learning in which an animal learns not to respond to a repeated stimulus.

Haversian system a unit of bone structure in which osteocytes (bone cells) are arranged in concentric circles.

hepatocyte a liver cell.

heterotroph an organism which requires organic substances as sources of energy and carbon; all animals and fungi are heterotrophs.

hippocampus part of the cerebrum which is partly responsible for the formation of new memories.

hypothalamus part of the diencephalon which helps to control the secretions of the pituitary gland, and also functions such as body temperature.

innate behaviour a pattern of inherited, pre-set behaviour that does not require learning or practice; also known as instinctive behaviour.

insight learning a type of learning in which an animal appears to integrate memories arising from two or more pieces of behaviour, in order to produce a new response that achieves a reward.

instinctive behaviour see innate behaviour.

iris a circular area of pigmented tissue that helps to regulate the amount of light that enters the eye.

Kupffer cells large, phagocytic cells found in the liver.

lactase an enzyme that catalyses the hydrolysis of lactose to glucose and galactose.

lacteal one of the lymphatic capillaries in a villus.

ligament a structure made of collagen fibres, that holds bone to bone at a joint.

lipase an enzyme that catalyses the hydrolysis of lipids to fatty acids and glycerol.

lipoprotein a ball made of lipids and proteins that enables water-insoluble lipids to be transported in blood plasma.

macula a patch of sensitive cells in the utriculus and sacculus of the inner ear, responsible for sensing position of the head.

maltase an enzyme that catalyses the hydrolysis of maltose to glucose.

mechanical digestion the breakdown of large pieces of food into small ones, by chewing and the churning produced by muscles in the walls of the alimentary canal.

medulla oblongata the part of the brain that lies immediately above the spinal cord, which controls breathing, heart rate and blood pressure.

meninges three membranes that surround the brain and spinal cord.

microvilli extensions of the cytoplasm on the surface of a cell, such as on the epithelial cells of the villi.

mucosa the inner layer of the wall of the alimentary canal.

muscularis externa layers of longitudinal and circular muscle in the wall of the alimentary canal.

muscularis mucosa a layer of smooth muscle in the mucosa of the alimentary canal.

myosin a fibrous protein that makes up the thick filaments in muscle.

neuromuscular junction a synapse between a motor neurone and a muscle fibre.

operant conditioning a type of learning in which an animal learns to carry out a particular action in order to obtain a reward.

opsin the protein component of the visual pigment of rod cells, rhodopsin.

optic disc the part of the retina from which the optic nerve arises, and where no rods or cones are present; also known as the blind spot.

ornithine cycle a series of reactions in which ammonia (from deamination) is converted to urea.

ossicle one of the three small bones in the middle ear.

osteoarthritis a degenerative disease in which the cartilage at joints becomes worn, increasing friction between the bones and resulting in loss of mobility.

osteoblast a cell that helps to form bone.

osteoclast a cell that helps to break down bone.

osteocyte a cell found in bone.

osteoporosis a degenerative disease in which the mass of bone gradually decreases, increasing the likelihood of bone fractures.

otolith a structure containing calcium carbonate, that lies on the receptor cells in the utriculus and sacculus in the inner ear and allows them to sense the position of the head.

parasympathetic nervous system part of the autonomic nervous system, whose neurones secrete acetylcholine as a transmitter substance.

pentadactyl limb a limb with five digits, such as found in amphibians, reptiles, birds and mammals.

pepsin an enzyme produced in gastric glands that breaks down protein molecules into shorter chains of amino acids; it is an endopeptidase.

peristalsis rhythmic muscular movements of the wall of the alimentary canal that push food along through its lumen.

plasma protein a protein found in blood plasma, such as albumin, thrombin or fibrinogen.

preganglionic neurone a neurone with its cell body in the spinal cord, whose axon terminates in an autonomic ganglion.

primary sensory area a part of the cerebrum which first receives information from sense organs.

receptor cell a cell that absorbs energy from the environment in the form of a stimulus, and transfers this energy into nerve impulses.

reflex a rapid, automatic response to a stimulus.

retina the part of the eye that is sensitive to light.

retinal the light-sensitive component of the visual pigment of rod cells, rhodopsin.

rhodopsin the light-sensitive pigment of rod cells.

rod a receptor cell in the retina of the eye that is sensitive to relatively dim light, but not to colour.

rumen a chamber in the alimentary canal of a cow, just before the true stomach, in which symbiotic bacteria break down cellulose.

saliva a watery liquid containing mucus and amylase, secreted into the mouth from the salivary glands.

sarcolemma the plasma membrane of a muscle fibre (muscle cell).

sarcomere one of many repeating units within a muscle fibre, stretching from one Z line to the next.

sclera the tough, white layer that surrounds the eyeball.

secretin a hormone secreted by the wall of the duodenum that stimulates the secretion of pancreatic juice rich in hydrogencarbonate (HCO_3^-) ions.

semicircular canals three fluid-filled canals in the inner ear that contain sensory cells that help with the sense of balance.

serosa a thin layer of connective tissue on the outer surface of the wall of the alimentary canal.

sinusoid a space between rows of hepatocytes in the liver, along which blood flows.

skeletal muscle striated muscle that holds muscles to bones.

somatic nervous system all of the sensory neurones in the body, plus the motor neurones serving skeletal muscles.

striated muscle muscle that has a striped appearance when stained and viewed under a microscope; cardiac and skeletal muscle are striated.

submucosa a layer of connective tissue lying beneath the mucosa in the wall of the alimentary canal.

sucrase an enzyme that catalyses the hydrolysis of sucrose to glucose and fructose.

suspensory ligaments ligaments that connect the lens of the eye to the ciliary body, and hold it in position.

sympathetic nervous system part of the autonomic nervous system, whose neurones secrete noradrenaline as a transmitter substance.

synovial joint a joint at which significant movement can take place between the bones; it is enclosed in a capsule lined with a synovial membrane that secretes synovial fluid,

tendon a structure made of collagen fibres, that holds a muscle to a bone.

tropomyosin a fibrous protein associated with actin in muscle, that covers the binding sites for myosin when the muscle is at rest.

troponin a globular protein associated with actin in muscle, that responds to the presence of calcium ions by changing shape and moving tropomyosin away from the actin–myosin binding sites.

trypsin an enzyme produced in the pancreas that breaks down protein molecules into shorter chains of amino acids; it is an endopeptidase.

vagus a cranial nerve that is part of the parasympathetic nervous system.

villus a finger-like process, about 1 mm in length, that increases the surface area in the duodenum and ileum.

visual acuity the sharpness of the image perceived by the brain; cones give greater visual acuity than rods.

visual pigments the light-sensitive pigments, rhodopsin and cone pigments (iodopsin) in the rods and cones in the retina.

vitreous humour a viscous liquid that fills the part of the eye behind the lens.

Index